Psychic Protection
Lifts the Spirit

Psychic Protection Lifts the Spirit

CASSANDRA EASON

quantum

LONDON • NEW YORK • TORONTO • SYDNEY

quantum

An imprint of W. Foulsham & Co. Ltd
The Publishing House, Bennetts Close,
Cippenham, Slough, Berkshire, SL1 5AP, England

ISBN 0–572–02645–5

Printed in Great Britain by St. Edmundsbury Press, Bury St. Edmunds, Suffolk.

Contents

Introduction

Though the popular image of psychic protection is of exorcisms in darkened churchyards and scattering circles of salt to keep off vampires, it is, in fact, an issue that touches most people's lives. Preparing yourself psychically for the day is no different from making sure that your mobile phone is charged and you have your season ticket and money before you leave for work. In the evening, shedding the negativity of the day is like taking off your work clothes and kicking off your shoes. When you are ready for bed, you lock the doors and check that the lights are switched off – so in the same way you should close down your energies to prepare for peaceful sleep and creative dreams. The bedtime prayers and lullabies of childhood served just this purpose.

In addition to the power of personal protection, we have to remember that we are all interdependent and if we work towards increasing the positive energies of the cosmos, we will benefit others as well as ourselves.

This book will explain every aspect of psychic protection in a relevant and practical way and show you how you can harness the positive energies around you to improve your life.

ONE

What is Psychic Protection?

We are all subject to countless impressions from morning till night, and while we sleep, many positive thoughts and emotions come to us from fruitful interactions with others, and from the thoughts, words and dreams of family and friends or a lover far away. However, less loving feelings can also invade our waking subconscious or sleeping mind; these may be deliberately malevolent, but it is perhaps even more likely that unconscious negative energies may be directed towards us. Someone may be sitting brooding in the daytime or lying awake at night seething with resentment against us because it appears that our partner is more desirable (and undeserved), our children healthier or more intelligent, our home more comfortable or our career more successful than their own. Then there is pollution – both actual noise and environmental disturbances – for we live in a frantic world of traffic fumes, faxes, phone calls and e-mails that intrude upon our consciousness both day and night. In these ways our minds and souls can become overwhelmed and the effects be manifest as stress, an inability to concentrate, a series of minor accidents or a general lack of energy. You may suffer from insomnia, nightmares, stress-related illnesses, or infections that are slow to clear.

Moreover, certain people you encounter either at work, at home or socially – whether a depressed colleague, a critical relative or an intrusive neighbour –

may mean you no harm but nonetheless seem to leave you feeling drained and make your nerves jagged. While they are not exactly psychic vampires, nevertheless such emotional leeches can regularly and routinely deplete your energy stores and offload their negativity on to you. Just think for a moment how different you feel after a lively encounter with a good friend, compared with the feelings you bring away from a stressful meeting with your least favourite colleague, and you will see exactly what I mean.

Some buildings, too, can make you feel tired or uninspired, especially tower blocks, warehouses and duplexes that lack natural light and ventilation or are built around a metal structure. Dowsers would say that there are black streams running beneath them, and I shall examine this theory later in the chapter on Travel and Workplace Protection (see page 165). Certainly, there are workplaces where there is constant conflict and a lot of stress-related illness. I have encountered this when a firm relocated into a new building and the harmonious atmosphere and creativity of the original workplace seemed to disappear overnight, to be replaced by back-biting and lethargy. In the same way, certain houses can be dark and gloomy even in summer; in particular rooms you may experience a sense of malevolence that is frequently interpreted as a ghost but may, in fact, be due to the darker energies of the land on which the house is built.

Such harmful influences may be caused by negative thoughts, deliberate spite or very occasionally spirit attack (ironically, this may well often be brought on by dabbling with ouija boards or calling up spirits *for fun*) – but they can all be replaced with positive energies. This actual transformation of negative into positive is crucial for psychic protection, for if you simply do away with the negative and do not replace it with anything else, you are leaving a gap for doubts and fears to return and the job is not complete.

Our early ancestors understood this principle instinctively and chose symbols that represented power and light to protect them from darkness and danger. They wove protective knots and made Mother Earth figures and spiral horns of plenty from the last sheaf of corn cut down at the first harvest at the end of July, known as Lughnassadh in the Celtic tradition. These benign but potent corn dollies, or spirits, were preserved in homes until the spring equinox, when they were buried in the fields to bring fertility to land, animals and people. Because they were ritually destroyed each year, we have no real idea how early this practice began, but certainly the forms still used in these corn figures resemble early Mother Goddess motifs and so they probably began with the Neolithic farmers in Northern and Western Europe. What is significant and what we can learn from this is that protection and fertility have always been recognised as two sides of the same coin – as are destruction and creation. Throughout the history of many cultures, the tradition has continued that the most powerfully protective amulets and charms also have life-giving qualities.

Banishing negative energies

Whatever the negative or draining energies directed your way, you have three forms of defence that in practice are interwoven: you can block them, or counter their negativity with even stronger positive vibes or, in the case of deliberate, malicious and unprovoked attack, return the energies to the sender.

In all these instances, the first step is to remove any negativity that has already reached you by using simple rituals involving candles, crystals, herbs, incense or the formal aura-cleansing methods that I describe in later chapters. Then it is important to erect a defensive shield at times when you know you are vulnerable: in a hostile work or social environment, when travelling, during divination or psychic work, when counselling others, caring for the sick and while you are asleep, which is when most attacks occur. Protective amulets are especially powerful in shielding you at times when you are most exposed, and if you regularly empower and cleanse them, they will become more effective over the months. They may even last for years if you preserve them carefully (see Protective Amulets, Talismans and Charms, page 36).

The home is an important area in which to establish ongoing protection, since it is here that we want to be truly open and receptive to the sorrows as well as the joys of our loved ones and to relax the barriers we erect during the day. You cannot be truly open in love if you remain behind a psychic shield, and so you need to ensure that negativity is left at the door, that your home is regularly cleansed of any anger or resentment after the quarrels, worry and sorrow we all experience. Bedrooms, especially those of children, benefit from regular crystalline protection and burning oils and herbs, while herbal baths will clear the stresses and frustrations that can all too easily leave us unable to sleep and so prey to dark thoughts during the night.

Once children go out into the world, psychic self-defence on their behalf can help to shield them from dangers from strangers, traffic and bullying. In addition, simple rituals can help the child to feel safe and powerful and therefore confident to face confrontation and hazards. Recall, for a moment, those little rituals that sports players perform before they serve a tennis ball or kick a penalty – three paces back, two little jumps and rub the right foot on the back of the left sock – they are simply personal, empowering rituals.

Finally, you can make a real difference to places that are suffering negativity and those areas of natural beauty that are under threat from deforestation or pollution. If we can clear the negative energies of our personal work space, whether we regard them as black streams or free-floating negativity, and defuse or dispose of our own natural annoyances and fears safely, rather than directing them to others, however they have wronged us, we can surely improve the energies of the universe, which are at root composed of the interaction of single atoms.

Making positive energies from negative

One of the oldest remedies for psychic protection is to leave sacred water by your bedside to absorb all negativity while you sleep. You can obtain special water from sacred wells that still exist in many locations or make it yourself from commercial mineral water drawn from a former sacred spring, for example Malvern spring water. The process is a very simple one, using a Celtic remedy. The Celts called crystal quartz 'star stones', because they were believed to be frozen stars.

- Find nine small quartz crystals lying naturally in a stream or on a seashore and rinse them in pure running water to remove pollution. Our ancestors did not need to do this, of course.

- Place the crystals in a litre/1¾ pints of the spring water or pure water, bring the water to the boil and then allow it to cool. The water has healing properties and so is very powerful for absorbing negativity. This will be sufficient water for nine days.

- Place a little of the water in a glass bowl by your bed last thing at night.

- In the morning, the used water may be poured on to a pot of fragrant, healing, flowering herbs such as lavender or chamomile and the pot placed where the plant receives the sunlight. In this way any negativity is transformed by the earth and light into a positive force for nurturing creation.

- Remember to make some more crystal water on the tenth evening.

This principle holds good for all psychic protection work and if you do something positive after every cleansing or banishing ritual, then you are creating the powerful positivity that makes you invulnerable to attack.

If you are attacked by negativity at work, whether personally, or by telephone or e-mail, keep on your desk a small bowl of spring water into which you have placed some amethysts. Whenever you feel malicious energies being directed at you, dip your hands in the water and sprinkle it over your face to cleanse away the bad feelings.

TWO

Beginning
Psychic Protection

There is little point creating psychic shields or carrying out domestic or workplace protection rituals if you are seething with hatred, envy or resentment – albeit righteous indignation – at your boss, your best friend, or your ex-partner. Of course we cannot turn off our negative emotions, nor should we seek to repress them as they are as much a part of ourselves as our positive qualities. Instead, we should learn to transform them into positive energy, a great catalyst for change and movement. In this chapter, we will look at some simple ways of banishing negative energy and replacing it with a positive, cleansing and energising atmosphere, so that you can start making psychic protection work for you.

Getting rid of personal negativity

A method I have used many times in my own life to banish personal negativity and have also demonstrated successfully to others involves binding and tangling the pain and anger in a symbolic thread.

This method is very ancient and can be used to collect the bad vibes of the family as they return each evening, if the pot in which you hold the binding threads is placed close to the front door. You can also keep a knot jar at work in a drawer or tool box . You will find that, by effectively binding an angry response, you are able to deal with each difficult situation decisively and without adding your own tensions, which serve only to cloud an issue and cause a response that, on calmer reflection, you might decide was not wise.

- Find a wide-necked, dark glass bottle or a deep pot. It is best to use a new bottle or jar each time one is full, so an old coffee jar is excellent for this as you will not mind disposing of it.

- You will also need some dark brown thread or wool, the colour of the Earth Mother. This provides a secure grounding and degree of common sense that can be important in magical work.

- Hold a length of thread and cut it with scissors or a sharp knife to a length that will accommodate the number of knots you feel reflects the intensity of your feelings at the time – some people will need only one or two knots to bind the emotions, others may need more. As you cut the thread, say:

Cut the chain that binds
Thus the power unwind.

- Name the injustice or anger for the final time and tangle the thread by knotting it as many times as you like.

- When it is knotted tightly and all the bad feeling is enclosed in it, place it in your bottle or jar, saying this age-old rhyme, the origin of which is lost in the mists of time:

Tangle the anger,
Tangle the pain.
By this knot
Make me free again.

- Add a sprinkling of sea salt for purification and put the lid on the jar or bottle as soon as you have placed the knot inside. Keep the bottle or jar closed to keep in the threads of negativity and open it only if you wish to add another knot.

- If the feelings return, repeat the ritual.

- Each time you tangle and tie a knot, do something positive, although not necessarily spiritual. You could burn a warming, energising oil such as orange or bergamot in an oil burner, cook a special meal, do some planting or weeding in the garden, tend an office plant, make a short phone call or send an e-mail to someone who is lonely or ill. That way you add to the cumulative positivity of the cosmos.

You can use this method for injustices and stresses great and small, but if a matter is especially inflammatory, tie together several threads until you feel the anger or resentment diminishing. This is not weakness, but clearing the decks either to resolve the matter calmly, laying it aside once and for all, or to postpone dealing with it until another day. You can also use your bottle to bind your fears and worries about any aspect of your life.

When the bottle or jar is full, add a sprig of rosemary or basil to transform the negativity into healing and push the knots well down into the jar. Dispose of it in an environmentally friendly way and start another.

You will find that if you continue this ritual over a period of months, it gradually begins to take longer to fill a bottle as your resistance to stress increases. You will find more information on banishing negative energy in the chapter on Domestic Protection (see page 24).

Auric protection

There are many sources of protection you can call upon, using your auric or biofield energy, to repel and shield you from external malevolence, whatever the source, and from your own fears that may seem particularly overwhelming in the early hours of the morning.

The following is a very basic method of utilising natural energies to strengthen the aura or psychic energy field that is said to exist around us all. The field is believed to be created by the interaction of natural magnetic and electro-chemical reactions, combined with the energies of the subtle or spiritual forces within the body. Because this energy is not static, but interactive, the aura reflects not only the essential person but their current emotional state.

This is a very active form of protection that will energise you for the day or evening ahead as well as keeping away all that wish you harm. The aura is usually described as bands of colour and though it surrounds the whole body is seen most clearly around the head. However, for viewing the personal aura, you can see this ethereal light or mist most easily around your hands, and as your hands move, so will your aura. You will find more information on auras as a means of maintaining psychic well-being in the chapter on Chakra and Aura Protection (see page 153). First you need to practise recognising the aura.

- Hold your hands against a dark background with the palms facing and almost touching each other, then move them apart quickly. Continue to move your hands together and apart and you may find the action becomes more difficult as the energies from the force field accumulate. You may actually see bands of greyish light extend from the fingers of one hand to the other, either externally or in your mind's eye. You can use your imagination to kick-start your clairvoyant vision.

- If you lower one hand about 15 cm/6 in below the other, you may now see diagonal rays connecting the fingers.

- Next, either by candlelight or perhaps natural twilight or early morning light, hold your hands in front of your face, palms facing away from you at a distance of about 60 cm/24 in, with your fingertips about 5 cm/2 in apart. If possible, use a plain white wall as a background this time, although as you become practised your psychic sight will operate in all conditions from brilliant sunlight to almost total darkness.

- Let your eyes relax: you may now see the greyness as a silvery-grey glow following the shape of your hands. This is the auric energy from your etheric body that is said to exist within us all. It is the part that leaves the physical body on out-of-body journeys and some people believe that it survives death.

- Take time to allow the aura to emerge. If you try this exercise daily for several weeks, colours will slowly appear and sparks may begin to flare beyond the silvery grey. This may appear in the air around you like a shimmering halo, which may be close to your body or anything up to an arm's length away. You may begin to be aware of the aura around your body, but for now concentrate on your hands.

- If you do not see the auric light, simply visualise it and in time your clairvoyant vision will take over. Remember that this is a psychic energy and many people only ever see it in their mind's eye; clairvoyance does use the same faculties as the imagination and is developed by using and expanding our natural imaginative abilities. Visualisation is just another name for focused imagination and can be very powerful in bringing what is in the mind into actuality – in this case auric protection.

Using auric protection

As soon as you feel you are ready to use this auric protection, you can begin to put it into practice at any time that suits you. It may be at the beginning of a new day, or when you need to go out after dark, or if you know you may encounter a difficult or draining situation.

- Sit comfortably on the floor or on a bed with your knees together and your hands in front of you with your palms facing each other but not quite touching.

- Move your hands gently apart, then together, until you feel the energy building and perhaps lights, sparks or colours appearing.

- Raise your arms above your head in an arch and see the light becoming brighter and forming an arch between your hands.

- Extend the arch downwards so your whole body is sealed in the light and continue to do this in sweeping movements, nine times in all, seeing the light as pure white or perhaps swirling rainbows as you become aware of the different layers of your aura.

- If you are going into a hostile or intrusive situation, you can shake your fingers until you create golden sparks. This establishes a force field that will repel – but only with a gentle tingling – any who invade your personal space.

In time and with practice, you will be able to activate this protection merely by visualising the light extending from your fingers. See it enclosing your whole body in a golden sphere and the sparks emanating from your aura, and you will find that people do take a step back as if they have encountered an invisible force field – which, of course, they have.

If you find the exercise difficult, surround yourself with a circle of golden candles, large enough for you to sit safely in the centre, and allow them to form your shield of gold.

Invoking protection from higher powers

In the past, people traditionally asked for protection from God or the angels – and in even earlier times from the Mother Goddess – when faced with danger or when undertaking any form of psychic work. More recently, some people have begun to identify protection from a benign source of wisdom and goodness as emanating from a higher, more evolved part of the soul located within us all; this is often called the divine spark.

In recent years, however, more and more people have returned to the medieval principle of regarding angels and archangels as actual benign beings of light existing on a higher plane, who will aid us if we call out to them. Whatever your view of this source of light and goodness, you can create a candle ritual to invoke the benign powers of the universe.

This form of protection is much gentler than the previous one and is excellent for quiet evenings or bedtimes, or for times when you want to carry out divination, some form of psychic work or meditation. It is also appropriate at times when you are alone and feel vulnerable. It will not only calm you but also fill you with gentle, harmonious energies so that your unconscious wisdom can come to the fore and guide you through quiet contemplation, perhaps by candlelight or through creative dreams in peaceful sleep.

The four most important archangels – whether you see them as actual or symbolic – can be invoked by means of a ritual to stand in each corner of the room: they are Michael, the Archangel of the Sun and the warrior; Gabriel, the messenger; Raphael, the traveller with his pilgrim's staff; and Uriel, the Archangel of Salvation.

The archangel invocation is described in detail on pages 18–19 and there are various ways you can adapt the ritual based on the individual qualities associated with the four archangels, which are outlined below. You can use crystals or candles in the appropriate colours to represent each of the archangels, or you may prefer to use tall white candles to create pillars of light if you see the energies of positivity in a more abstract way. You can also burn a suitable oil or incense (see pages 20–21) for extra protection if you feel that you are under attack either psychologically or psychically. This is also a particularly good ritual to carry out before you travel, especially for a long period or overseas, as the protection is long-lasting.

Michael

Sometimes called the Archangel of the Sun, Michael is the archangel of light and the warrior angel. He appeared to Moses as the fire in the burning bush and saved Daniel from the lion's den. As commander of the heavenly hosts, Michael, usually pictured with a sword, drove Satan and his fallen angels out of the celestial realms. The angel of judgement, he also carries a scale weighing the souls of the dead. According to the Quran, the holy writings of Islam, the cherubim were created from Michael's tears.

Michael's traditional position is in the south with the noonday sun and he offers power to overcome any obstacles, wisdom, illumination and also challenge to find the right path. His colour is gold and his crystal is a citrine or pure crystal quartz. His incense is frankincense and his oil is orange.

Gabriel

Sometimes called the Archangel of the Moon, the messenger archangel or the heavenly awakener, Gabriel appears many times in the Bible. Most people will know of the episode when he visited the Virgin Mary and her cousin Elizabeth, mother of John the Baptist, to tell them that they were to bear sons who would lead mankind to salvation. He is usually pictured holding a sceptre or a lily. To the followers of Islam, Gabriel is the spirit of truth who dictated the Quran to Mohammed.

Gabriel stands in the west, bringing wise words of truth and the clear voice that speaks of hope and a new purpose in life, but he also brings compassion and the acceptance of the weaknesses of self as well as others. His colour is silver. His crystal is the moonstone or fire opal and his incense and oil are jasmine and mimosa.

Raphael

Raphael is the travellers' guide and the angel who offers healing to the planet and to mankind and all creatures on the face of the Earth, in the skies and in the waters of the Earth. He is also guardian of the young. Raphael is usually depicted with a pilgrim's stick, a wallet and a fish, showing the way and offering sustenance to all who ask for guidance.

He stands in the north and offers physical or emotional healing and reconciliation and also an awareness that there must be endings if there are to be beginnings. His colour is green, his crystals jade and aquamarine and his incense and oil are myrrh and pine.

Uriel

Uriel, whose name means 'Fire of God', is associated with earthquakes, storms and volcanoes, and is known as the Archangel of Salvation. He warned Noah of the impending flood and led Abraham out of Ur. Believed to have given alchemy to mankind, he also imparted to Hebrew mystics the wisdom of the *Kabbalah*, the oral tradition of Hebrew esoteric wisdom that formed the basis of spiritual and magical writings and practices.

Uriel stands in the east and offers clarity and a fresh perspective, but he may also herald necessary change. His colour is scarlet or orange, his crystals carnelian and amber and his incense and oil are sandalwood and rosemary.

The archangel invocation

There are many variations of this ritual for different purposes, for example empowerment or healing. This one seems to work well for healing. You can, if you wish, burn an incense in each of the four compass positions associated with the different archangels. These need not be exact directions but can be symbolic, although you can use a compass to find north accurately if you prefer.

- First face east, the direction of the dawn, the rising sun and spring.
- Light a red candle, calling upon the transforming energies of Uriel:

> Great Uriel, archangel of change and transformation,
> protect me from those who seek to bind me
> in destructive or redundant patterns or relationships,
> and from my own fears of the unknown, untrodden path forward.

- Face south, the direction of the noonday sun and summer.

- Light a golden candle, calling upon the light-bringing powers of Michael with such words as:

  Mighty Michael, archangel of light and power, protect me with your mighty sword from those who attack, undermine and seek to destroy my happiness and self-esteem, and from my own cowardice that holds me back from moving from the shadows into the light.

- Face the west, the direction of sunset and autumn.
- Light a silver candle, calling upon the wise counsel of Gabriel, the messenger, saying:

  Wise Gabriel, guard me against those who would manipulate my emotions and lead me into dangerous or destructive ways, and from my own weakness and carelessness in following the easy path and allowing others to shape my destiny.

- Face finally the north, the direction of midnight and winter.
- Light a green candle, calling upon the healing wisdom of Raphael, saying:

  Gentle Raphael, with your healing staff,
  protect me from spectres of the night and troubled spirits,
  those earthly vampires who drain me of vitality, and from
  my own night terrors that are more fearsome than any external peril.

- As you gaze at the light, create a psychic short-cut, so that you can activate the protection at any time you need it, for example by touching your third or psychic eye in the centre of your brow or making a cross on your hand, either the Christian cross or the cross of the Mother Goddess (the kind we see on hot cross buns), the old astrological sign for the Earth. As you do so, say:

  When I make this sign, I will instantly reawaken the power of the Archangels of Light to protect me.

Repeat the ritual every four weeks, or more frequently if you are undergoing a challenging or stressful period.

Oils, herbs and incenses

The easiest and fastest way of cleansing negativity and preventing it from permeating your home or personal space at work is to burn a purifying fragrance. Many of the protective fragrances have restorative as well as cleansing powers, and for thousands of years, in many countries, people have hung protective herbs or flowers in their homes or used fragrances for protection, cleansing and healing.

According to the Gaia hypothesis – named after the Greek goddess of the Earth and proposed by James Lovelock, a British biologist, in the early 1970s – the Earth is a self-regulating system, and within the herbal kingdom are all the cures for our ills, even those created by humankind. We can access some of those cures through natural fragrances.

In my chapter on Psychic Protection in Nature (see page 67), I shall describe in detail these different fragrances and suggest ways of using them. However, for now I have simply listed a few you can try as you begin to understand and use psychic protection. Burn the more potent ones in those areas where you go about your daily routine, where you work or study, reserving the gentler ones for rooms in which you relax or sleep. You can vary the fragrance in the bathroom according to whether you are preparing for the day or winding down in the evening. These fragrances are particularly effective if you have to face a difficult situation, say giving an important dinner party or entertaining a difficult visitor. The aroma will not attract comment, but you will find that conversations are less confrontational when a soft fragrance is used and that the mood of a gathering can be lifted by an energising fragrance, while all the time the scents are providing protection against unkind words or pessimism.

Oils

Oils can be used in various ways to enhance protection, cleansing, soothing and energising. **However, it is important to note that many oils are contraindicated during pregnancy and breast-feeding or if you have specific medical conditions. Always check with your doctor or a qualified practitioner.**

The following are all powerful protective burning oils.

Cedarwood: This fragrance is both soothing and uplifting, replacing negativity with optimism.

Cypress: Burned with lemon or geranium, cypress brings healing as well as cleansing.

Peppermint: Both a purifier and a cleanser, this oil can bring love and enhanced mental powers as well as removing negative energies.

Rosemary: Similar to peppermint in its effects, rosemary is a very positive oil for psychic protection.

Sage: Another oil with similar qualities to peppermint.

Thyme: Cleansing, purifying and stimulating, thyme is also similar to peppermint in its effects.

Bathing in protective oils

Having a bath in a gently protective oil – no more than ten drops in all – is also a good way of banishing the stresses of the day and opening yourself to love and gentle communication during the evening. Aromatic baths are also gently uplifting and so can be used in the morning if you need a gradual release of energy rather than a rush of adrenalin.

Protective bath oils include chamomile, geranium, lavender, rose or sandalwood.

Use of oils during pregnancy

Please note that **many oils should not be used during pregnancy**. Gentler oils, which can be used as alternatives, are chamomile, geranium, lavender, pine, rose or sandalwood. However, **none of these can be used in the first three months of pregnancy**. My advice, therefore, is that you should consult your doctor or midwife before contemplating trying any of them.

Herbal protection

Bay, basil, lavender, parsley and rose are particularly effective for protection. Make an infusion of one of them by adding about 15 ml/1 tbsp of the crushed fresh leaves or flowers or 5 ml/1 tsp of dried herbs to a cup of boiling water and leaving for ten minutes before straining and leaving to cool.

- Sprinkle a few drops in the corners of a room where you will carrying out spiritual work or divination, or in your bedroom before you go to sleep.
- Sprinkle a few drops over a child's or lover's bag before he or she leaves for work or school and on your night clothes if you are away from home.
- Sprinkle a few drops across the threshold of a room to prevent hostility from entering.
- You can also use the infusion to cleanse every room in your house, beginning at the front door and then working from the top of the house down, if there have been any domestic upheavals that have left bad feelings or unresolved conflict.

Incenses

Incense has moved beyond the field of ceremonial magic and is increasingly burned in homes, much as candles are, to create a relaxing atmosphere as a natural prelude to psychic work, and to banish negativity. The incenses that seem best to induce psychic awareness carry with them natural in-built protection.

Incenses are also a good way of cleansing a home of bad temper or unfair criticism that has engendered resentment and hurt. My favourite defensive and divinatory incenses are: cedar, dragon's blood, frankincense, gum arabic, juniper, myrrh and sandalwood.

Use cones, sticks or a small incense charcoal burner, any of which can be bought from candle shops or New Age stores.

In pregnancy, you may prefer to use chamomile, frankincense, lavender and sandalwood, as these are more gentle although still powerful. Again, it is best to check with your doctor or midwife first.

Slowing or closing down your energies

One of the most effective ways of marking the end of a concentrated period – whether of psychic exploration, stress or frantic activity – is to set aside a transition period. When I was a child in the late 1940s and 1950s, families would have a bath at the end of the day (in many homes, my own included, taking turns in a tin tub in front of the fire); they would then clear up for the night, then sit by the fireside with a mug of cocoa. This period of quietness helped everyone to wind down and relax and to reduce the night terrors and insomnia experienced by increasing numbers of adults and children today.

If you have been carrying out a magic ritual, divination or other form of psychic development, spend a few minutes quietly tidying your equipment and cleansing your crystals under water. Putting away everything in its special box or drawer or cupboard, and closing it, is a physical signal that you are putting this aspect of your world to one side for a while.

At the end of the day, you may also find it helpful do what our grandmothers and their mothers did: spend a few minutes tidying away clutter, followed by a simple supper or drink. Then sit quietly in candlelight, letting the day ebb away, after which you can have a bath in a protective fragrance to remove the final traces of the day. As a bonus, this also avoids the horror of waking to unwashed dishes and clutter that can slow down the positive energies of the new day.

Preventing tension escalating and restoring calm

If machinery or a computer is overheating, the cure is simple: you switch it off for a few minutes. In the same way, if you find yourself going into overload, you need to switch off too. If you don't, your efficiency plummets, your heart and pulse race and you will gain nothing but stress by continuing. So here is a simple ritual which has the effect of switching you off for a few precious moments to cool down.

- Whatever you are doing, stop. Sit or lie down and close your eyes, allowing the hum of your inner machinery to slow, quieten and fade so you are left inside a cocoon of quietness and stillness.

- Listen while any voices, telephones, traffic or other noises recede as though down a dark tunnel – you can even allow yourself to fall asleep for a few seconds.

- When you are ready, open your eyes, blink and let the sounds and bustle slowly return. Now imagine that events around you are taking place on a video that you can control. Turn down the volume and slow down the speed so that life continues with less momentum.

If you experience a stressful phone call or meeting at work, try to spend a few minutes alone to calm the mounting tension you feel. Remember, if you leave it unchecked, it may make you increasingly enervated and likely to make mistakes that will only make your panic or stress levels rise further.

If possible, spend a few minutes in the open air to restore your connection with the Earth. This will absorb any negativity, reconnecting you with basic root energies that can help to set any problem in perspective and allowing your survival energies to kick in. Touch the grass, soil or pavement or whatever is under your feet, and stamp three times to release the darkness into the Earth, saying or thinking this mantra:

It is gone, it is done, I am one.

If you are cooped up in a high-rise office building, a ride in a lift to the basement can re-establish this connection with the Earth. Use this ritual to help you. There is more information on grounding techniques in the chapter on Everyday Psychic Self-defence (see page 138).

- As the lift descends, let the anxieties rise and float away from you. Close your eyes and see the darkness flowing from your head, down your body, through your arms and legs and through your feet. Get out at the basement, stamp your feet three times and repeat the mantra:

It is gone, it is done, I am one.

- If possible, walk back up the stairs and when you return to the room where the tension occurred, immediately do something positive: make a phone call that will make you feel good or do some essential job that you have been avoiding.

All these simple rituals will give you a greater understanding of psychic protection and how you can use it in your life to improve the way you feel about yourself and your surroundings.

THREE

Domestic
Protection

Psychic protection was practised in the home long before it was given its current name or became a specialist subject. Dion Fortune, who founded the Community (later the Fraternity) of the Inner Light that was originally part of the Golden Dawn esoteric movement, formalised the concept in 1930 in her book *Psychic Self-defence*. But domestic protection against negativity has been practised for thousands of years, although originally dark influences were attributed to malevolent spirits or witches.

Psychic protection is sometimes thought of in terms of spirit attack or deliberate malevolence from others (see pages 114–24 on Psychic Protection Against Attack). However, most protection involves removing the negative traces of the day to avoid carrying your irritations into the home where they may clash with the residual irritations of other family members. In this way, you can enjoy harmonious relationships and quiet sleep at home, so that when you encounter the new day you feel energetic and psychically strong.

When our forebears scrubbed out their homes and polished the doorsteps, they were carrying out fundamental but powerful psychic cleansing. As my late mother always said when we came home from school: 'Leave your muddy shoes at the door so you don't tread the day through the house.'

The knot pot I suggested in the previous chapter serves the same purpose, forming a barrier for anger entering the home, or indeed the workplace.

Protective boundaries

Humankind has always drawn defensive boundaries and lit fires around dwellings to keep away animal and human predators and also malevolent forces from beyond the physical world. Even the crowded terraced houses of Victorian England had their small yards or gardens surrounded by a high fence or wall. Modern open-plan housing estates and apartments with communal areas lack the natural boundaries that designate an area as our private place. However, even if you only have a balcony or a small area outside your door, you can erect your protective barriers.

Originally these barriers are likely to have been thorn-bearing trees and bushes and trailing plants or vines that entwine malevolence. It is no accident that Thorn, the most protective rune, is named after the thorn and bears its shape. Bay, palm, myrtle, juniper and rowan trees also formed protective boundaries. (See pages 69–85 for lists of protective plants.)

Rowan, or mountain ash, is especially good for protecting the home and outbuildings. Planted by the garden gate, it helps to keep out unwelcome visitors. Rowan crosses, made from branches that are not cut with a knife or any metal, and tied with red twine with nine knots, can be placed on the outside of a garage, garden or bicycle shed to deter thieves and vandals.

The garden, balcony or yard can become your sanctuary, and green or trailing plants mark out your domain, a haven of privacy. This is where you can retreat to after a hard day that ended with you travelling home on a crowded train or bus or in a traffic jam of angry commuters.

Plants placed just outside your front door will also absorb the emotional garbage of the day, but do remember to tend these plants as they are working so hard, and rotate them – perhaps with ones outside the back door or on your window ledge – so they can rest and be restored. Place moss agate or jade in the soil around your defensive greenery to strengthen them and use a spray containing a few drops of a protective flower essence: try the Bach flower essences agrimony, larch or oak, all-purpose Glastonbury thorn essence, the Deva elixir fig tree or Findhorn bell heather or thistle (see also Everyday Psychic Self-defence, page 138).

A defensive flower bed or window box could include basil, cumin, wild garlic, parsley, rosemary, sage, thyme and vetivert, while the cacti you see out of doors in warmer climes are frequently placed at the four corners of a property to repel psychic or worldly invasion. Bamboo is another protective plant; bamboo canes, especially if tied with red cord, can hold up roses or bean plants and tiny outward-facing mirrors to disguise your magical intentions from intrusive neighbours, while keeping them firmly on their own side of the fence.

Sacred guardians

In the traditions of both East and West, every home had a protective guardian or household deity. It was often the wise ancestors who were believed to protect the family and this belief still exists in Africa and Asia.

In Chinese homes today, the kitchen god, Tsao-wang, the god of the stove or hearth, is represented by a picture on paper rather than a statue. This image is placed in a small wooden temple over the hearth, facing south. Tsao Wang Nai-nai, his wife who is pictured next to him, carries the sayings of the women of the household to the Jade Emperor, the ruler of the heavenly court and principal deity in popular religion. Each morning three incense sticks are burned in the domestic shrine.

In ancient Rome, the *lares* and *penates* presided over the dwellings and affairs of the Roman households. The *lares* were deified ancestors or heroes and the *lar familiaris* was the spirit of the founder of the house who, it was believed, never left it. The *penates* were chiefly the gods of the storeroom and guardians of the home who protected it from outside danger. Their statues had a corner of honour in each house, and wine, incense, cakes and honey were offered to them at family festivities.

Animals, too, both mythical and actual, have been invoked to guard the home. The Chinese placed stone lions outside public buildings and believed that at night they would come to life and guard the property.

In Europe and Scandinavia, ward sprites, or personified Earth powers, were regarded as the natural guardians of settlements. They were said to assemble each evening at a crossroads near the centre of a village or town and pass along the old fairy paths towards hills or watch posts, where they would stand sentinel against all that was malevolent, earthly or otherwise.

Creating shadow guardians

There are many dangers, especially from intruders at night in urban areas, and fears of other-worldly attack are also magnified as darkness falls. If you live alone or spend nights by yourself, you may wish to create your own guardian of the household. This may be the statue of an animal. I have a large, dark, ceramic model of Bast, the ancient Egyptian goddess who took the form of a cat, and another of Tauret, the Egyptian goddess usually represented as a pregnant hippopotamus, both of whom offer special protection to women. These stand facing my bed. However, you may prefer to have a stone lion or a griffin, a mythical creature with a lion's body and an eagle's head and wings that dates back into antiquity, outside your door. Other people may prefer to have a figure with spiritual significance: the Virgin Mary, the Mother Goddess, Buddha, Ganesh, the Hindu god of children, or an archangel.

Our ancestors would, when darkness fell, send their fiercer guardians – such as Bast or a lion or tiger – out in shadow form to roam around the boundaries and repel enemies. And if you live in a dangerous area, you may well feel that such a potent guardian might help you to sleep in comfort and security, especially if you have young children or an elderly relative to protect as well as yourself.

You may like to have a powerful statue to calm more extreme fears and a gentle one for quiet protection. If you are given your statues as presents or choose them during a happy holiday or excursion, they will be naturally endowed with positive emotions.

Fresh seasonal flowers or greenery, especially if still growing, will naturally empower your statue with protective energies. You can cleanse it by burning a pink candle regularly on either side to absorb any fears or anxiety that may have been transmitted to the figure by your own fears.

The following is a method you can use at night to protect either your own home or that of a vulnerable friend or relative.

- Take three large, very pure white or natural beeswax pillar candles and arrange them in a semi-circle in a darkened room with a slight breeze (a light wall background works best). You may be able to buy beeswax candles shaped as angels. Beeswax is especially protective as bees were a symbol first of the Mother Goddess and later of the Virgin Mary. Experiment, so that when your candles are alight they cast huge shadows on the wall and with the flickering flame they appear to move.

- As you light each candle, say:

  Light my way safely, keep my home and the homes of those I love from darkness and danger.

- Stand your personal protective power statue in front of the candles. Use an angel statue and smaller pink candles to reassure children and help them to sleep free of night terrors. Again experiment with the positioning of the statue so that you can extend its shadow over a large area and even cast a halo of light over the figure.

- Visualise the shadowy form enclosing your home or that of a loved one.

- As you gaze at the shadows, say very softly, over and over, like a mantra:

  Go far, roam free, not to harm, but as guardian of my home,
  to turn back all who come with malevolence in their hearts
  and to defend from the perils of the night.
  Watch until daylight returns.

- When you see the gentle shadows all around, blow out the candles and say:

  Depart and remain afar, all you that would harm or disturb
  the sanctity of this dwelling place.

A fibre optic lamp in pastel colours is also a good way of diffusing light around a room and works wonders for nervous people and insomniacs.

Protection from theft and intruders

Natural substances such as minerals are frequently used in magic and ritual. Iron is naturally protective for homes and I have written about it in detail in Protective Crystals and Metals (see page 87). I first came across this ritual in Wales when I went there on holiday as a child more than 40 years ago. However, since demonstrating this on television, I have made various adaptations on the suggestions of viewers who knew similar rituals.

- Find a small metal box – you may come across a metal money box or old-fashioned nail boxes in a garage or car boot sale. It is worth searching because if you can find one made of iron, this is best of all.

- Fill it with old nails, the rustier the better, screws and, most importantly, a key from the household – not a front or back door key, but one from a drawer or an old cupboard.

- Sprinkle the contents with rosemary, rue and fennel – freshly gathered, if possible, as the living energies are more protective than the energies in dried herbs. If you cannot obtain these herbs, substitute some with similar properties (see the chapter on Psychic Protection in Nature, page 67).

- Bind up the key, knotted tightly with red twine in nine knots, and add it to the box last of all, saying:

  Key of my home, of all I love,
  Bind with iron chains my sacred hearth,
  'Gainst those who come with ill intent,
  But those in need find welcome.

- Close the box and place an iron chain with a padlock round it. Use an old padlock and as you close it, throw away the key.

- Wait until it is dark on a night of the waning moon, then bury the box in your garden and tell no one where it is. If you do not have a garden, place the box in a basement, an attic or in a storeroom on a high shelf.
- Do not try to identify the place in the morning.

Witch bottles

Witch bottles, or protective dark glass or stone bottles, are common in many cultures and ages. They were filled with protective substances and buried outside the front doorstep or under the foundations of a new home. Witch bottles are traditionally made in bright sunlight to endow them with positive energies that are then sealed in the bottle.

Here is how to make a basic witch bottle.

- Three-quarters fill your bottle with a dark liquid, such as red wine or vinegar. Alternatively, use sacred water from a holy well or water from a running source that you have left in sunlight and moonlight for 24 hours from dawn on the day of the full moon until the next dawn when the lunar energies are at their most powerful and the moon rises at sunset. Since the moon and sun are on opposite sides of the earth and in opposite astrological signs, it is the time of a catalyst for a surge of power.
- Add a pinch of sea salt to the liquid when the sun is high in the sky, making the sign of the cross, either the Christian form or the cross of the Mother Goddess (see page 19).
- Into the liquid, drop iron nails and screws, some bent into the shape of a lucky horseshoe.
- Finally, add a sprig of rosemary, vervain or dill and cork your bottle firmly or screw the lid tightly. Seal it with red wax.
- Bury your bottle in a sealed container deep in a flower bed near the front of your house, or if you have a doorstep sunk into earth, place it under that. Otherwise, store it as near to the front of the house as you can, perhaps in the front eaves of an attic. If you live in a flat, you could erect a very high shelf near the door that can only be reached by a ladder.

A *planetary protective ritual*

Some people prefer not to bury a bottle once and for all but to have a living, protective focus, and this is especially good if you live in a flat.

This ritual draws upon the protective energies inherent in each of the five ancient planets that have been visible to the naked eye since time immemorial, plus the Sun and the Moon.

- Take a very large glass or ceramic bowl or a bottle with a very wide neck, the kind used for creating indoor bottle gardens.

- Fill this with soil and in it bury seven tiny moss agate or jade crystals, saying for each one:

  Bless my home and all who dwell therein from danger, anger and harmful strangers.

- Next, select seven fragrant protective herbs, one to represent each of the ancient planets. Seedlings are better than seeds as the protection operates from the beginning. You can use either the herbs I suggest here or use those listed in the section on protective herbs in the chapter on Psychic Protection in Nature (see page 67), and adapt your ritual accordingly.

- Take first rosemary, a herb of the Sun, dig a small hole in the soil and as you plant it, say:

  Protective light of the Sun, bring warmth and illumination to my home and those I love.

- Next, take lemon balm, fragrance of the Moon, and say:

  Protective light of the Moon, endow your fertile, restorative energies on my home and those I love.

- Next, take lavender, herb of Mercury, and say:

  Protective light of Mercury, guard my home from thieves and bring healing to those I love.

- Next, take eau de cologne, herb of Venus, and say:

  Protective light of Venus, bring love and harmony to my home and those I love.

- Next, take mint, herb of Mars, and say:

  Protective light of Mars, remove stagnation and bring courage to my home and those I love.

- Next, take sage, the herb of Jupiter, and say:

  Protective light of Jupiter, bring only wise words and kindly justice to my home and those I love.

- Finally take thyme, herb of Saturn, and say:

  Protective light of Saturn, enclose and endow security upon my home and those I love.

- Leave the herbs in the bowl or bottle by the door until they grow tall. You can, if you wish, transplant them into the garden.

Seasonal cleansing

In earlier times, domestic protection was largely ongoing and each season had its sacred plant or herb. At the midwinter solstice it was holly, the origin of the holly wreath on the door at Christmas. On May Day, it was a rowan cross tied with red twine and hung on outbuildings. At midsummer, a circlet of the herbs trefoil, vervain, St John's wort and dill, which bloomed at this time, was hung on the door or scattered around thresholds (see also the chapter on Psychic Protection in Nature, page 67).

New Year

All cultures use water and perhaps fire to purify homes for the New Year. Whenever the New Year falls in the calendar of that land or religion, dirt is swept out of the home, signifying the removal of bad luck and old sorrows. The basic concept is to drive all the bad fortune away and attract positive vibes. This is sound psychology as well as magical practice, as all the old disappointments, cynicism and unfulfilled dreams are symbolically washed away or burned.

In many parts of the UK, the old calendar is burned at sunrise on New Year's Day. Wind a piece of red wool nine times round the calendar, then throw it into the flames and say:

Old year burn, old troubles do not return.

But this ritual need not be confined to the actual New Year. If you have had a particularly bad month at any time, you can use the page of the previous month's dates on a tear-off calendar and burn it on the last day of the month at midnight, slightly adapting the old rhyme to say:

Old month burn, old troubles do not return.

Write down something positive to do the very next day, something that will give you pleasure.

Until quite recently, in Scotland on New Year's morning, all exits from the home were sealed and juniper berries burned in the hearth. The home was thereby purified for the coming year so that good fortune would follow. A more acceptable and environmentally friendly ritual involves burning incense and you can do this not only at New Year but at any transition period in your life, or any time when you have experienced a run of misfortune or unfriendliness.

An incense ritual for protecting a home and cleansing it of negativity

Use three cedar, three juniper and three pine incense sticks placed in a very deep heatproof container so that you can carry the incense round the home. The three groups of three are very significant: their total, nine, is the sacred number of completion. If you cannot get these incenses, substitute a cleansing fragrance from the section on protective herbs and flowers (see pages 76–85), but remember to exercise caution as I mentioned before if you are pregnant or suffer from any medical condition.

- Light each incense stick separately.

- Slowly turn the container nine times anti-clockwise, then nine times clockwise, saying until you have finished:

> One brings love, two stops danger
> Three and four from foe or stranger,
> Five takes bad luck clean away,
> Six lets good fortune only stay,
> Seven, eight and nine new hopes tomorrow,
> Three by three, thus be gone sorrow.

- Carry the incense into every room: begin at the front door, then go first upstairs if there is an upper storey, beginning from the top left of the house to the top right, then downstairs from right to left, ending at the back door. Repeat the chant in each new area. If there is a basement, cleanse it immediately after the ground floor, returning to the back door.

- Place the incense near the front door to burn through and bury the remains in a small wooden box with a sprig of fresh rosemary and some iron nails for protection.

- Afterwards, open windows and doors and introduce seasonal flowers and greenery growing in pots, an excellent source of *prana*, or the life force, to let in the new energies.

Sweeping magic

The time around the spring equinox on or around 21 March was traditionally the time for cleaning out the home after the long winter, although in colder climates this might be postponed until May Eve. Until 1582 in Europe, and 1752 in England, New Year's Day was on 25 March and the two cleansing periods merged. The most popular form of spring-cleaning and one that has entered the magical traditional of witches is sweeping, and even in modern rituals some witches use traditional besoms for sweeping out the area to be used for magic.

The broomstick has always been used in magic because it was part of every home and it is only in recent years that folk magic has borrowed from the more formal ceremonial tradition and required separate artefacts for ritual. In fact, the older concept of using household items and natural substances for magic carried with it in-built protection.

The broom was kept behind the door with the bristles upwards to drive away bad spirits and even today many people, myself included, when leaving home, leave the kitchen or garden broom bristles uppermost to deter thieves and vandals.

Couples not married in church were said to live 'over the brush' because they jumped over a broom as part of the pagan handfasting ceremony, said to be a potency and fertility symbol because the bristles and handle represented the union of female and male!

A *sweeping ritual*

Sweeping an area in anti-clockwise circles, having scattered dried lavender over the floor, is an excellent way of removing negativity. As a less energetic, but equally effective, modern substitute, you may prefer simply to add the lavender to the dust bag of your vacuum cleaner and hoover up in anti-clockwise circles, finishing by hoovering clockwise to re-energise each area of your home.

But if you have matters in your life you want to banish, perhaps old resentments or angers, bad habits such as smoking or over-eating that are causing you unhappiness, a minor but chronic illness in a loved one, or even lethargy, you can symbolically sweep it out of your life. While you should not try to banish a person, you can remove the negative aspect of them that disturbs your well-being, such as gossip, back-biting or anger, using the following ritual.

- Write what it is you wish to banish on six pieces of paper, six being the number of harmony. Each time you write the word or phrase, make your writing smaller, until on the last piece of paper, the writing is scarcely visible.

- On each piece, cross through what it is you wish to banish and then tear the papers into tiny pieces and drop them on the floor, saying for each piece:

Out with sorrow, out with pain,
Joyous things alone remain.

- Scatter lavender, rose petals or pot pourri on top of the papers and then sweep the paper away from you towards and through the back door, or suck it up in a vacuum cleaner, saying:

> *Dust to dust, away you must.*
> *New life bring, welcome spring.*

- If you have no back door, you can clear the paper with a dustpan and brush and dispose of it in an external waste bin.

- Remember to shake your broom afterwards in the open air or replace the dust bag in the vacuum cleaner.

A *group sweeping ritual*

If you are working with friends on a joint venture, for example to reduce noise and dust from building works or pollution in your area, or are helping each other to quit bad habits, you can do a sweeping ritual together. You will need a broom for each person in the group.

- Each of you must write a phrase or word as before on six pieces of paper and rip up your papers, but this time drop the pieces in a large pot or vase and add the lavender.

- Then together tip over the pot, saying:

> *Thus we banish, from our sight*
> *What no longer can be right.*

- Each person in the group must hold the handle of their broom in one hand and the bristles of another person's in the other, to create a circle of power. Circle slowly nine times clockwise, chanting faster and faster:

> *Three times three, the power I raise,*
> *Bringing with it happier days.*

- Finally sweep to the four corners of the room or yard, chanting as before, but now six times for harmony:

> *What is not right cannot bring joy,*
> *Thus we do its thrall destroy.*
> *Dust to dust, away you must.*
> *New life bring, welcome spring.*

You will probably end up laughing and that is best of all, because joy dissipates doubts and darkness faster than anything and it is only over the last 30 years that folk magic has become serious and separate rather than part of the rich tapestry of human experience.

Scrubbing away negativity

In cultures of African origin, there are many variations of cleansing rituals in which salt and pepper, both protective and energising substances, are added to water. The solution is used to scrub the back and front doorstep (or the nearest part of the home to the outside world) before sunrise to keep harm away from your home and its inhabitants all day. The secret is to scrub outwards, and then to throw away the water towards the rising sun, still before sunrise. Salt and black pepper sprinkled on the floor and then swept up and burned are also said to keep away any who wished you harm. In European-based cultures, scrubbing is also considered magical, but fragrant herbs are added to the water.

Scrubbing may also be used to remove lingering bad feelings or negativity, especially your own – for example after a quarrel or an outburst of temper from a family member, neighbour or friend. I often think that it is not surprising that many of our forebears who routinely used 'elbow grease' in the days before wonder household mousses and gels had less need for therapists and counsellors. Simple chants like the one below were also a feature of domestic magic possibly because, like children's playground songs that had their origins in folk magic, they were easy to remember and so to pass on. Peppermint, parsley or valerian infusions can be used to wash floors or yards.

- Add half a cup of dried herbs to 1.2 litres/2 pints/5 cups of boiling water, leave it to soak for five minutes, then strain off any herbs that have not dissolved. Alternatively, use eight or nine drops of lemon, geranium or tea-tree essential oil in a medium-sized bucket of water.

- As you add the oil or herbs to the hot water, stir the water clockwise nine times with a long wooden stick from a healing tree such as ash or hazel, saying another of the counting rhymes as you stir:

> One for joy, two for gladness,
> Three and four to banish sadness,
> Five and six flee useless anger,
> Seven, eight, nine remain no longer.

- Then scrub anti-clockwise with an old-fashioned brush – brilliant for reducing tension – or with a mop, reciting:

> Nine, eight, seven, six, five, four, three, two, one,
> The spell is done,
> Sorrow (or anger) begone.

FOUR

Protective Amulets, Talismans and Charms

Amulets or protective charms have been carried or worn in all cultures and times to offer protection against physical and supernatural danger, misfortune and illness. The first amulets were probably small painted stones; examples dating from prehistoric times have been discovered at the foot of rock-painting sites in Western Canada. Talismans have the same protective powers, but in addition are actively empowered to attract good fortune, love and prosperity to the bearer. The terms tend to be interchangeable nowadays.

Many amulets derive their powers from nature and so crystals or gems are worn or carried for this purpose since they contain innate healing and protective powers. Metals are also regarded as inherently protective as they come from the earth, itself perhaps the most powerful protective force (see the chapter on Psychic Protection in Nature, page 67) and many amulets are crafted from or engraved on metal. Another common type of amulet or talisman was made from part of an animal, and was designed to transfer the animal's salient quality or strength to the possessor, while also endowing them with the protective strength of the creature.

From ancient times, people also crafted amulets and talismans of tiny figures representing gods, sacred animals, arrows and tools. Indeed it was suggested that jewellery originated as the wearing of amulets made of lucky or healing stones.

Chinese parents still follow the custom of giving their children jade to protect them and keep them healthy, and in many countries coral jewellery is worn by young children to prevent falls. Coral and bell teething rings, given at christenings and naming ceremonies in both the Eastern and Western worlds, are said to ward off negativity and nightmares. In India, most amulets are still – as they have been for thousands of years – created from sacred plants.

In some cultures, for example that of Ancient Egypt, amulets not only guarded a person during life but were placed in the tomb for protection in the afterlife; protective hieroglyphics (magical letters) were painted on the tomb walls and placed as amulets on the mummy.

Magic bags

Magic bags are a popular feature of many cultures and have survived in many indigenous or inherited magical traditions. Though these bags are sometimes given negative connotations in films about voodoo, they are strongly protective as well as empowering. Like all magic, they can be used by a practitioner as a focus for negative as well as positive intent – but since cosmic law dictates that all energies return threefold to the sender, in such cases the sender will receive a magnified negative response.

Magic bags include the Native American and African medicine bags and bundles, the Afro-American mojo bag and the European and Scandinavian charm bag.

In Europe until the Industrial Revolution, country people would fill a small red bag with a pinch of salt, a piece of cloth, a tiny lump of coal, a silver heart or silk cut into the shape of a heart, a silver sixpence and a piece of bread. The bag would be sewn up in red thread or tied with a red drawstring thread and the words chanted nine times:

> This bag I sew [or carry] for me
> And also for my family,
> Let it keep through every day,
> Trouble, ills and strife away,
> Flags, flax, food and Frey.

The flagstones in the last line referred to a home, flax to clothing, and Frey was the old god of fertility in Northern lands. The contents of the bag echoed the European and Scandinavian New Year first-footing ceremonies. The salt was to protect the household against illness and psychic attack, the coal ensured there would be sufficient fuel for the winter, the heart symbolised love and family harmony, the sixpence promised enough money, and the bread sufficient food on the table. Red was the colour of Frigga, the Norse Mother Goddess and protectress of the household.

The medicine bundles possessed by all tribes in the Native North American tradition contained an assortment of objects with magical and healing powers. Some held only a few objects while others could hold over a hundred, including charms, herbs, hooves and feathers. Small medicine bundles were possessed by individuals as well as the official medicine men and women. The contents were often dictated by dreams and visions and the official bundles would be opened before a special event or ritual as symbol of the releasing of their power. There were special bundles associated with major ceremonies, for example the Crow Indians' annual Sun Dance. This dance was outlawed in the nineteenth century, partly in an attempt to westernise the Indians, but was relearned in the 1930s and has been revived in recent years. Tribal medicine bundles were passed down by their guardians, and individual ones were buried with their owners or bequeathed to a chosen relative. Some medicine bags still surviving today contain objects that are more than 200 years old and even natural substances are perfectly preserved.

You can put almost anything in your personal protective/empowerment bag, and the more personal the items and the greater the positive emotion endowed in each one, the more potent it will be. Some people begin magic bags for their newborn children and add mementoes of their early life, including holidays, and small treasures that mark milestones over the years. Sometimes these bags are handed to the child when he or she enters adolescence, leaves home, gets married or becomes a parent. However, you can create your own medicine bag at any age and add to it at different stages to reflect your evolving self. If any area of your life becomes unfruitful, you can return the representative symbol to the Earth, casting a feather to the winds from a hilltop, or a shell or stone into the sea. You can carve a tiny personal symbol on a piece of wood you find, or paint a symbol on a special stone or shell you discover, to mark the beginning of a new stage and add it to your bag.

Making your magic bag or medicine pouch

First choose a small bag or pouch made from any natural fabric. In it place about six objects that are of protective significance and seem to bring you luck and confidence. An item may combine protective and luck-bringing properties or you can choose three protective and three empowering objects to preserve the balance. The chosen items may be small treasures, for example charms that you have had from childhood, a feather from a bird that symbolises freedom or power, hair from a horse's tail, a favourite crystal or stone you found on the beach on an especially happy holiday, a pressed flower given by a lover, or a small china animal of the kind that seems to embody qualities you admire or strengths you desire.

A bead is a common addition to a personal magic bag in several cultures. Blue beads especially are traditionally associated with repelling the evil eye, as you will see in the chapter on Protection Against Psychic Attack (see page 114). Beads are also associated with spiritual power in many religions, such as Catholicism and Buddhism. In these traditions they represent a prayer or significant teaching and so if you handle your bead regularly, you will receive all the accumulated positive energies. Some people use a bead from a necklace they were given for a special birthday or one that commemorates a happy anniversary; however, you can simply choose a bead that feels right from a craft or jewellery store.

Small stones that are found by the sea, especially those with a hole in the middle – symbols of the Mother Goddess in her oceanic guise – offer healing, as well as granting glimpses through the orifice of other dimensions. Lucky coins, too, can protect against financial loss and encourage prosperity, again especially those with holes in, for example Chinese divinatory coins.

Because all these objects are endowed with positive memories they will protect you in times of trouble or uncertainty and will increase in positive power as you use or carry them. You may want to add a tiny sachet of protective herbs, for example dill, basil or lavender (see the chapter on Psychic Protection in Nature, page 67) or the bark from a healing tree such as ash or aspen.

Many native cultures, such as the American Indians, the Aborigines and the Maoris, believe that we are each linked with a species of animal, bird, fish or even a tree, flower or herb, the special qualities of which are mirrored in ourselves. Spend some time choosing your special objects so that they reflect not only what you are but what you would like to become.

Mark your medicine bag or pouch with the glyph of your zodiacal Sun sign (see pages 43–6) or a personal symbol of protective power. I have made some suggestions later in this chapter but you may choose perhaps a significant symbol from a recurring dream. You can either embroider this on your bag or write it in an indelible gold or silver pen.

Do not let other people use or handle your bag because it is an expression of your inner self and so is precious. Keep your bag with you during the day when possible and sleep with it close to your bed, as your own personal symbolic repository of the power and protection that is within you and is daily amplified by the natural world.

The mojo bag

In spite of its exotic and sometimes frightening reputation, a mojo bag is remarkably similar in purpose to the medicine bag, and the word is itself a corruption of the term magic. Mojo bags come from the Afro-American tradition and are generally made of red flannel, but can be in different colours or even occasionally made of leather.

Mojos are always carried – sometimes around the neck on a cord, sometimes round the hips or in a pocket – and are kept out of sight. Those protecting homes or work premises are kept near the door, again unseen, as it is believed that if a mojo bag is touched by someone else, it loses its power and luck.

Empowering your magic bag

You can either bless and empower each item separately or place them in the bag and perform the ritual over the whole bag, which may be easier and is equally effective. Since you are creating a protective as well as empowering focus, transition times are especially potent, for example one of the equinoxes, solstices, the day of the crescent moon or when one star sign period changes to another. Work when the sky is full of light.

- At any of these times, place your bag or the individual objects on a purple cloth, the colour of wisdom and spirituality.

- If possible, take your bag to a sacred place, such as an old stone circle or standing stone, or close to running water. However, you can perform your ritual equally well in your garden, on a balcony or indoors close to an open window through which the air circulates.

- If you are working outdoors, scatter a few grains of dry earth or sand over your bag (so that it will brush off easily). As you do so, face north and say:

Mother Earth, grant me protection and power,
so that my thoughts and actions are rooted in kindness.
I ask you to empower this bag as a symbol of myself.

- Next, face east and, holding your bag skywards to catch the breeze, say:

Father Sky, grant me protection and power,
so that my thoughts and actions are free from prejudice and limited horizons,
I ask you to empower this bag as a symbol of myself.

- Next, face south and hold your bag in any sunlight – during a Moon period, the crescent moon should be pale in the sky – saying:

  Brother Sun, grant me protection and power
  to replace the darkness of sorrow or anger with the creative fire of
  inspiration. I ask you to empower this bag as a symbol of myself.

- Finally, face the west and sprinkle over the bag a few drops of water, if possible from a running source or rainwater that has not touched the ground before collection, saying:

  Sister Water, grant me protection and power always to move forward,
  washing away regrets that bind me to the past
  and fears that hold me back from embracing the future.
  I ask you to empower this bag as a symbol of myself.

If you are working indoors, you can use salt to represent Earth, incense for Air (Sky), a candle flame for the Sun, and water in which a crystal quartz has been soaked, for the running water.

If bad things or negative emotions occur, as they will in any life, rededicate your bag or add an amethyst or rose quartz for a while to remove any negativity, washing the crystal afterwards under running water. When good things occur, open your bag to the sunlight or moonlight to absorb the positive feelings.

If you can share any good luck or prosperity that comes your way – not only with family and friends but also with anyone who is genuinely in need of good fortune – you are adding positive vibrations to the cosmos. When you need a boost of luck or money for yourself, you can tap into these accumulated energies. Think of this as a kind of cosmic savings bank.

Making a good luck bag

If you have had a run of bad luck or just left an unhappy relationship, then make yourself a special good luck bag, with a small golden object for the power, energy and confidence of the Sun; a silver charm or object for the intuitive wisdom of the Moon; and a copper or coin for Venus, who brings love and money. You could also include a clear quartz crystal. These were regarded in earlier cultures as pure creative energy and in Japan and China were called the essence of the dragon.

Also add a small dark crystal such as smoky quartz or obsidian (Apache tear) for protection, and something living, such as a pressed flower, or a twig from a magical tree such as hazel, hawthorn or rowan. In addition you may wish to choose something personal, perhaps from your childhood, that symbolises the essential person you once were and will be again.

For a time, carry both bags so that the good luck will rub off on your personal medicine bag. When things improve, leave your good luck bag in a high place where it is open to sunlight and fresh air for a few days. Then wrap it in white silk, adding an amethyst to restore its energies and allow it to rest in a drawer until you need it again.

Amulets and talismans

There is something very magical about creating your own talismans and amulets from wood, stone, clay – found naturally if possible – or crystals, marked with the astrological glyph of your Sun sign (see pages 43–6), perhaps interwoven with that of your birth ascendant sign if you know it. You could also make your initials into a pattern, or write or draw a single word which you feel is symbolic of your personality.

Some people use initials of their secret power names, the name you choose for yourself that embodies those special qualities you possess or would like to own. Witches choose a name by which they are known in the craft, but tell only those they can trust, as it was said that to know this secret name was to have power over you (which I do not believe to be true). Nevertheless, this name is very special and Native North Americans would acquire their name from the animal, bird, insect or plant that offered them wisdom on their solitary initiatory quest as they reached adolescence. Think about this name and if you are a closet eagle, lion or embryo goddess Diana, express this on your protective/power charm.

Making an amulet or talisman is remarkably easy and you need not have any great talent for art and crafts. A simple symbol painted or drawn with a waterproof pen in red, the Viking colour of magic, on a stone found on a shore, endowed with all your hopes and wishes, is more powerful than an expensive amulet bought from a New Age store, because the power lies in the meaning with which it is empowered.

However, you may surprise yourself at how gifted you are and find that you can engrave wood with a pyrography set from an art shop, or with the blade of an awl or screwdriver heated in the flame of a gas cooker. With stone or metal, you can use an awl or sharp screwdriver to etch a shape in the surface and then fill in the outline of the symbol with paint.

You can use a stone with a natural hole and hang it from a cord around your neck, or drill a small hole for a cord in a special stone or shell, or buy a small silver clamp to hold the stone or a crystal on a chain. Some people believe that you should not drill holes in crystals and by the same token you should not use stones if they require cutting or shaping; but I think that is to endow the crystal with human feelings, which would exclude some of the finest and most spiritual sculptures from being created. If you prefer, you can carry the stone or crystal in a small pouch with you. Stones from or near a source of free-flowing water are especially potent and round wooden discs can also be made into talismans, cut from a fallen tree branch or even an old broom handle. If you varnish the wood on both sides, it will last for years.

Traditionally the week before the midsummer solstice is a time for making protective amulets so that they can be passed through flame on the solstice day at noon or held up towards the solar disc. Old amulets are traditionally burned or buried on Midsummer Eve, but like me you may not like a period between the old and new amulet, or may choose to keep your amulets for several years.

If you do want to replace your amulets annually, you can wear or carry both your amulets, the old and the new, from Midsummer Eve and then, having empowered the new one at noon, remove the old one and bury it as the sun goes down on the most powerful day of the year. However, if you want to make amulets at other times of the year, choose the day of the full moon and empower them at noon. You can then bury old amulets when the full moon is first visible in the sky (check your diary or the weather section of a newspaper if the weather is cloudy).

Personal talismanic signs

As I have already mentioned, the most powerful symbol of personal identity and thus very protective is the glyph of one's birth sign, interwoven, if you know it, with your ascendant sign, the sign that was rising over the horizon at the moment of your birth. You can paint the symbol on wood or stone, or engrave it on metal. Alternatively, you could create a set of 12, perhaps on stones or the appropriate crystals listed below, and carry the glyph symbolising the particular strength you need at a particular time. For this reason I have listed the additional protective powers and empowering qualities for each glyph. You can carry your birth glyph as well to help to connect you with your essential self.

Empower each amulet by passing it nine times through the listed coloured candle, facing south at noon on the day of the full moon.

Aries

The ram, 21 March–20 April. Protects against cruelty, anger and aggression; brings courage, assertiveness and impetus for positive change.
Candle: Red　　　　　　　　　**Crystal:** Carnelian or jasper

♉ Taurus

The bull, 21 April–21 May. Protects against material loss, debt, eating disorders, infidelity and free-floating fears; brings prosperity, patience and strength if the way ahead seems hazardous.
Candle: Pink **Crystal:** Rose quartz

♊ Gemini

The heavenly twins, 22 May–21 June. Protects against thieves and deception of all kinds, illness and confused thoughts, trouble with siblings and neighbours; brings clear communication, versatility and logic.
Candle: Pale grey or yellow **Crystal:** Beryl or agate

♋ Cancer

The crab, 22 June–22 July. Protects the home and family, and travellers, especially at sea or by night, against terrors of the night, supernatural attack and problems with a mother or mother figure; brings fertility and intuition.
Candle: Silver **Crystal:** Moonstone

♌ Leo

The lion, 23 July–23 August. Protects against physical danger, risks of all kinds, unwise passion and excess of all kinds, bullies and autocratic behaviour by others; brings joy, confidence, energy, power, good fortune and nobility of spirit.
Candle: Gold **Crystal:** Citrine or topaz

♍ Virgo

The maiden, 24 August–22 September. Protects against unfair criticism, spite and jealousy and any who would destroy your self-esteem; brings good health, efficiency and the ability to discern people and things that are of worth, striving for perfection and for healing powers.
Candle: Green or pale blue **Crystal:** Jade

Libra

The scales, 23 September–23 October. Protects against injustice, crime, inertia and unbalanced emotions in self or others and relationship difficulties; brings balance, inner harmony, love and karmic resolution.
Candle: Blue or violet   **Crystal:** Lapis lazuli

Scorpio

The scorpion, 24 October–22 November. Protects against hidden enemies, personal predators, those seeking revenge, violence, sexual cruelty and poltergeist activity; brings second sight, strengthens personal auric field, regeneration and the restoration of what is rightfully yours in any area of life.
Candle: Burgundy or red   **Crystal:** Malachite or bloodstone

Sagittarius

The archer, 23 November–21 December. Protects against accidents, unprovoked attacks, pessimism and prejudice; brings clarity of vision, open-mindedness, joyous travel and the widening of horizons.
Candle: Yellow or orange   **Crystal:** Turquoise

♑ Capricorn

The goat, 22 December–20 January. Protects against intolerance, incompetence, procrastination and attacks from officialdom, including banks, schools, government departments and the medical profession, disloyalty at work and from family, trouble with a father or father figure; brings stability, security, wise caution, loyalty and prudence.
Candle: Black or brown   **Crystal:** Garnet

♒ Aquarius

The water carrier, 21 January–18 February. Protects against coldness in relationships, being abandoned, from exploitation by those who have no principles, from false friends and unfulfilled dreams; brings idealism, impartiality and independence.
Candle: Indigo or dark blue   **Crystal:** Aquamarine

Pisces

The fish, 19 February–20 March. Protects against confinement of all kinds, restrictions, chronic ill-health, criminals, illusion, conflict of loyalties and priorities and unhappy endings, especially those forced by others; brings spiritual awareness, intuition and sensitivity to the feelings and needs of others, transformation and new beginnings.

Candle: White or mauve   **Crystal:** Clear crystal quartz

Universal magical signs

Magical symbols which date back to palaeolithic times span several cultures and have over the millennia accumulated collective energies from all those who have drawn or painted them or invoked their protection and power. So when you use them you are in a sense activating a psychic short-cut to their power, healing and wisdom.

The following protective/empowerment icons are some that I have collated from a number of sources during the years I have been writing on the paranormal. This is by no means a comprehensive list but all the symbols are easy to reproduce and in the case of very simple ones can form the basis for a personal motif made by combining a basic shape in a number of different ways. They are all light-bringing and have transcended the culture of their origin to guard us today against the dangers of modern society as effectively as they once did the hunter–gatherers who drew them on cave walls or etched them on bark. Because the greatest protection lies in joy and health, you will find that the amulets do make you naturally happier and more confident, and attract good fortune as well as repelling harm.

Ancient amulet symbols

Mother Goddess symbols

The first Mother Goddess images come from 20,000 years ago in areas stretching from the Pyrenees to Siberia, and magical signs of the protection and fertility of the Mother have continued throughout different religious and magical traditions. The basic shapes of these early amulets have become the basis for later magical and religious symbols of all kinds.

These symbols are gently protective for men and women, and tend to release slow-acting but long-lasting nurturing energies. From neolithic times, zig-zags were painted on jugs and on stones or early jewellery to represent the Mother Goddess renewing life with falling rain. So zig-zag patterns can help to clear negativity caused by stagnation, repetitive redundant energies and destructive relationships or life patterns, and protect against depression. If you use waterproof paint and a non-porous material, you can dedicate this amulet by taking it into the rain.

Lunar discs

The first lunar discs were engraved on mammoth teeth as early as 2000 BC and were sacred to the Moon Mother in all her aspects. The Crescent Moon talisman that appears in pagan art has been absorbed into the Christian faith and is shown in fifteenth-century paintings and on statues beneath the feet of the Virgin Mary. The Moon symbol protects travellers and seafarers and guards against supernatural malevolence and night terrors; lunar amulets are especially good if you or your child sleeps badly.

Butterflies

Butterflies are also associated with early Mother Goddess magic. The butterfly is an image of regeneration more recently associated with the sixteenth-century Spanish mystic, St Teresa of Avila. It can, however, also be found as a symbol of regeneration on neolithic vases from the fifth millennium BC – and again on stones and jewellery. The butterfly guards the home or wearer against ill fortune, sorrow and loss of all kinds.

Bees

The bee was another image that survived from these early times and reappeared in Christian tradition. The hive was likened to the womb of the mother. The followers of the Greek Corn God and Demeter, the Mother Goddess, were called *melissae*, Latin for bees, and as I mentioned in the previous chapter, beeswax candles were used in both pagan and Christian religion. Bees, like butterflies, offer the benevolence of the Mother Goddess's protection and are good for children, babies, pregnant women, mothers, very elderly or sick people, and for protection against loss, rejection, loneliness and grief. Butterflies and bees are such gentle images they can be worn day or night.

Spirals

The spiral, associated with the womb and new life, was a very early charm for fertility and joy. Ammonite fossils which contain the spiral shape can be bought quite cheaply from museums or mineral stores or can sometimes be found on beaches. They represent the spiral or pathway to enlightenment and will protect against all forms of malevolence, cruelty and violence and shield you from a sense of hopelessness.

Male protective symbols

Just as men can quite happily wear the female symbols of protection, so the later hunter or Sky God icons can offer safety to women. However, they do have stronger, more directed energies and so can be used for a more immediate threat or if courage and strength are needed to resist attack.

Symbols of male energies of power and courage developed with the onset of the hunter–hero gods of the early Bronze Age, and the earliest icons were antlers or branches with sprouting leaves overlaid with crossed hunting staves. These protect against all forms of physical attack and danger and also against cruelty and deliberate malice.

The Mother Goddess spiral evolved into the snake, which forms a male phallic symbol of potency and strength. Snakes are closely associated with rebirth and regeneration, because they shed their skin in the spring.

The double entwined snake of the classical Hermes and Mercury's caduceus, often a living, growing staff, are both symbols of healing and of powerful communication. The snake forms two circles, the interlinked cycles of good and evil, life and death, light and darkness. The wings on the caduceus are for wisdom, so this can guard against gossip and malicious words as well as illness. By association with Mercury, who was, among his many patronages, god of moneylenders and thieves, it can also protect against poverty and trickery.

Medieval alchemists portrayed the ouroboros, the snake swallowing its own tail, a symbol of endless cycles of time, birth and rebirth unbroken. Because of the shape it promises long life and protects against infidelity and all destructive, divisive forces.

However, the simplest magical symbols are geometrical ones. Two of the most common are the Sun and the Earth.

The Sun symbol is a circle with a dot inside, which is also used as the astrological sign for the sun. The circle represents spirit and the whole cosmos, everything that is. The dot is the seed of new life, the limitless given form. This is a potent symbol of ambition, career, success, energy, action, and making dreams come true. It protects against all forms of darkness, both earthly and spiritual, despair and depression, and also all who would do evil under cover of night.

The Earth symbol, a cross within a circle, is a potent symbol for protection during any form of psychic work and from free-floating fears. It offers grounding against panic that can turn a one-off accident or setback into a spiral of bad luck (see also the chapter on Everyday Psychic Self-defence, page 138). You see this type of cross on hot cross buns, an example of a pre-Christian symbol that subsequently entered Christianity. The idea was that as you ate the food, you acquired the energies and fertility of the Earth. This symbol, which is still the astrological sign for the planet earth, stands for fertility, money, practical achievement and domestic harmony. It can be used in homes and if you want to reverse bad luck you can turn the amulet so that when worn it forms an X.

Egyptian hieroglyphic amulets

The power of the hieroglyph, the pictorial symbol for different letters or words in Ancient Egypt, is that each pictogram is in itself a repository of protection and potency that could be drawn up simply by drawing the symbol or invoking its name. As I mentioned earlier, hieroglyphs were painted on tomb walls or placed on mummies to offer their specific protection to the dead on each stage of their journey to the afterlife.

The Eye of Horus

One of the most famous symbols is the Eye of Horus, which has over several millennia and in different cultures retained its potency against the evil eye or curses.

Horus was the Ancient Egyptian Sky God, represented as a falcon or a falcon-headed man. His eyes were the sun and moon and his wings could extend across the entire heavens. He was frequently associated with the morning aspect of Ra, the Sun God, and worshipped as Re-Harakhte.

The hieroglyph represents the white or Sun (Ra) eye, and marks the full power of the sun. Therefore it is empowering as well as protective and guards against deception since it is the eye of truth. Though comparatively few people now believe in the evil eye, nevertheless this icon is regarded as one of the most potent against all forms of malevolence and psychic attack, deliberate and unconscious.

The vulture

The vulture represents the protection and power of the divine mother Isis, and was used as protection for the deceased with Ankh, the key hieroglyph for life engraved on each talon. Isis demonstrated the power of maternal protection when she cared for Horus in the marshes and protected him from his evil uncle Set, or Seth, who would have destroyed him. So although this may seem quite a frightening image, it is one that does carry universal love and if engraved under a child's bed or placed over their bedroom door, offers protection even when you cannot be with them. It is also good for any family members who travel away and anyone who is vulnerable in any way.

Shen

Shen represents the orbit of the sun around the earth and so was a symbol of time. As an amulet placed upon the dead, it promised eternal life as long

as the sun endures. As such, it is another very protective amulet against illness, accident or despair, fears of ageing and the ending of happiness or a permanent relationship. Therefore it is a good amulet to give to someone with whom you enter a permanent commitment. On a home it can protect against storms, hurricanes, typhoons and earthquakes.

Ankh, Wedja and Seneb

These three hieroglyphs are frequently used together to symbolise life, prosperity and health and could form either a design of a single amulet or be part of a triple amulet, perhaps three small crystals on a cord. In the tombs of a pharaoh, the three signs, Ankh, Wedja and Seneb, were written after his name, endowing eternal life, prosperity and health in the next world. So it is an excellent protector to give to anyone setting out in the world, moving to a new home, emigrating or making a major life change.

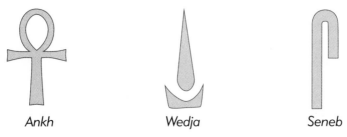

Ankh   Wedja   Seneb

Ankh, the key, is the symbol of eternal life. Pictures on tomb walls show an ankh being held to the nose of a pharaoh (the nose was thought by the Egyptians to be the source of life), thus ensuring that he would continue to live after death. As a single icon it is also highly protective against all forms of danger and instability, both in the physical world and in people's emotions.

Wedja, or Fire, was used by the Ancient Egyptians to forge metal, smelt gold and create the beautiful pieces of jewellery for which they are famed. The hieroglyph was based on a bow drill which turned in a shaped piece of wood (the lower part of the hieroglyph) to produce fire by friction, and so Wedja came to represent prosperity and any means of money-making or creating material security. It is therefore good as a talisman for good fortune, as well as protecting the wearer from financial loss, bad luck, depression and inertia, whether in oneself or other people.

The symbol for **Seneb** was the first letter in the Egyptian word that means 'health' and has come to represent the whole concept of health and well-being. It is very empowering in all health matters, and will protect those with poor health as well as anyone who is going to a place with poor hygiene and health care. It also guards against stress and psychosomatic conditions.

Magical symbols

The Seal of Solomon

The Seal of Solomon is perhaps the most magical symbol of all with its six-pointed shape integrating two sacred triangles that represent the number three. Three, of course, is a number imbued with great significance in many religions and cultures. The Egyptians had their sacred trio of Isis, Osiris, the Father God, and Horus, their son. The Celtic icon, the Triple Goddess, was from Neolithic times associated with the Lunar Goddess in her three phases: maiden, mother and wise woman, or crone; the Roman goddess Diana appeared similarly in three forms (Diana Triformis). Christian religion is based on the Three in One, the Father, Son and Holy Ghost. And there is, of course, the inner triplicity of the human being: the mind, body and spirit.

Bind runes

The Vikings and Anglo-Saxons regarded their sacred runes as containing power, much in the same way that the Ancient Egyptians saw hieroglyphics as sources of energy rather than mere letters. Runes – angular magical symbols etched on wood, stone and metal – were used on inscriptions or in divination and were adapted in different forms through many lands of Scandinavia and Western Europe until the coming of Christianity.

Bind runes are considered especially magical and consist of two or more runic shapes joined to form a single symbol, thereby amplifying the powers of the separate runes. These sometimes appear in ancient inscriptions, carved on jewellery or objects.

For example, the rune **Thorn** represents a thorn and the hammer or the might of the Thunder God Thor, or Thunor. When combined into a bind rune with **Ur**, the rune of primal strength, the rune of the herds of wild cattle whose horns the Vikings wore in their helmets, it forms a symbol of might that will protect against any danger and shield from attacks of any kind. It also endows the wearer with the strength to survive and thrive.

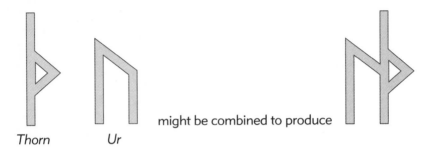

Thorn Ur might be combined to produce

This particular bind rune is quite commonly found, but there must have been many others. Unfortunately, the majority of runic inscriptions and amulets, especially those carved on wood, were lost in the passage of time. It is therefore a mistake to put forward these forms as the only right ones, as some runic writers do.

Bind runes are essentially a creative art and best devised by an individual for a specific need. Often other runic forms will appear in the combination that add to the energies, and runes can even take on additional meanings when placed in conjunction with one another.

A *bind rune for restoring fertility*

If your energies are blocked or there are stagnant issues that leave you feeling fearful or drained of energy, you can form this bind rune to remove them and allow fertile restorative energies to flow into your life. It can also be used to assist physical conception.

You can combine two or three from those listed in this section (or the books in the back) to create a motif.

For example, **Ing** represented the autumn/winter period when the land and people rested before the planting of the new crop. It was drawn on the side of houses to offer protection, especially from inclement weather, and was also a fertility rune.

Gyfu, the rune of the gift, refers to sexual unions and marriage as well as creative giving and so is a good rune for banishing loneliness or a sense of alienation.

To this design is added a third rune, **Beorc**, the rune of the Mother or Earth Goddess, named after the birch tree that seeds itself, and thus a source of self-regeneration – powerful stuff.

A combination of these runes comprises the ancient fertility trinity: Ing, the father, Beorc, the mother, and Gyfu, the union and ultimately its product. I have drawn one example of how they might be combined.

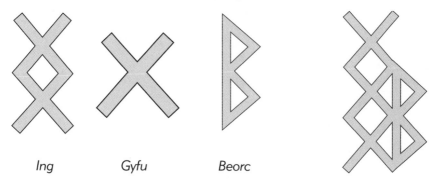

Ing   Gyfu   Beorc

You can join the three individual runic forms in different ways, upside down or horizontally, to create your own unique focus of energy. Everyone's fertility bind rune is and should be different. You can even make a repetitive pattern design of the three main fertility runes.

A *bind rune for financial security*

You can also create a bind rune for protection against financial loss or poverty, and to bring prosperity and material security.

This example also combines three runes, the first being **Feoh**, the wealth rune.

This links with **Gyfu**, the gift, in the sense that it says whenever you give willingly without hope of reward, your generosity will be returned threefold.

The final rune included in this bind rune is **Wyn**, the rune of personal happiness, whose joy comes from maximising every moment of happiness.

The combination of Feoh, Gyfu and Wyn could be combined to create a bind rune such as this.

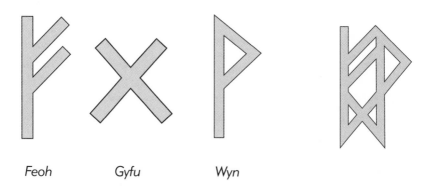

Feoh   Gyfu   Wyn

A *bind rune for good health*

This bind rune will protect against illness and maintain or restore health and harmony. First use **Eh**, the rune of the horse, which represents harmony with others and integration of different parts of the self.

The second rune in this combination is **Aesc,** the ash tree. This is the tree of healing, of endurance and strength.

This final rune, **Ur,** represents primal strength.

These three could combine to create something like this.

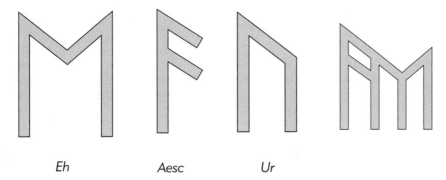

Eh   Aesc   Ur

A *protective bind rune*

This bind rune is designed to protect the home and family from external attack and internal quarrels, bringing happiness and security at home.

Odal is the rune of home and domestic security.

Beorc is the nurturing Mother Goddess.

Ger is the rune of the harvest and the bringer of abundance.

A combination of these three could create a bind rune something like this.

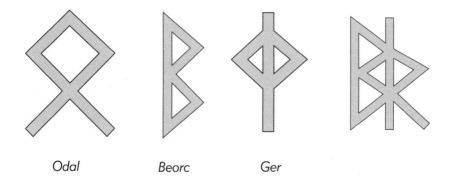

Odal   Beorc   Ger

A *bind rune for strengthening your identity*

If you are in a situation in which you need to strengthen your identity against earthly malevolence and psychic attack from any source, you can also create a bind rune to protect you.

Ac, the oak tree, is sacred to the Viking Father God Odin and Thor the Thunder God, and is a tree associated with the power of the Sky Gods.

Peorth, the Destiny Rune, represents the core essential person within us all.

Cen is a Fire Rune, the torch of pine that cleansed and illuminated the dark halls of the warriors.

So these three runes can be combined to create a bind rune something like this.

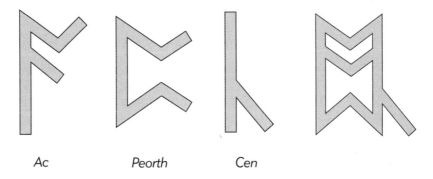

Ac   Peorth   Cen

Word *charms*

Words and numbers have long been associated with magical protection and power, and again are a very easy way of creating a personalised amulet or talisman. Traditionally, these word charms were created in wax or written on parchment and worn in a tiny bag around the neck or carried in a pocket. Sometimes parchment charms were kept in tiny silver tubes.

You can also create a parchment or wax charm for a lover or family member and they make a lovely gift for a newborn baby. You could make one on a tiny circle of high-quality parchment or paper and fit it inside a locket or hollow gold or silver medallion.

You can buy parchment from craft stores or mail order outlets or you can sometimes obtain tiny pieces of ready-cut parchment from a New Age store for talismanic purposes. However, with care, you can cut it with tiny cuticle scissors. You can also buy parchment kits complete with tools, pens and instructions. This ancient art is currently enjoying a revival and it will serve well for all your magical work – and enable you to make lovely cards for special occasions as a bonus. More information is contained in Further Reading (see page 179) and Useful Contacts (see page 182).

However, you can also use good-quality paper and waterproof inks or paints for making number and word talismans or, if you are skilled at needlework, embroider them on fabric.

You can make a larger wax charm from several candles or a parchment scroll amulet for your home or workplace. Keep it above a door frame or in a box in a drawer or hidden behind a picture – these written amulets are best kept out of sight to work their magic, not least because the curious may handle them and imprint them with scepticism or false fears derived from watching too many bad B-movies on the occult!

Wax protection amulets

Wax amulets are especially potent because they have been created from the four ancient elements: Earth, represented by the candle itself; Air, seen as the smoke rises; Fire, in the flame; and Water, in the melting wax. The union is said to create a fifth element, Akasha, or Ether, that is captured in the wax tablet.

Wax protective amulets and talismans were made for many different purposes, one of which was to confer invisibility on the wearer. This was not meant literally but signified that an aura or mistiness, in modern terms, was cast around the subject, so that those who might do harm would not be aware of their presence. This ability can be very helpful: it may be useful, for example, to have a low profile at a meeting at work when someone is seeking to offload blame for a mistake or omission. In a new workplace, too, or a social situation, where there are many potential conflicts or interrelations that are not immediately obvious, it can be as well merely to observe initially before interacting. You can create wax amulets for different purposes or have a single general-purpose one.

If you wish to assert your essential self openly, however, at a time when your identity or abilities are under attack, you can also engrave one of the symbols listed earlier on wax or use your zodiacal sign.

Making a magical wax protection amulet

Usually darker colours are used for wax amulets: deep purple for wisdom and spirituality; brown for the Earth Mother; a deep green, Venus's colour, to enfold yourself in love; or dark blue for the protection of the ancient Sky Fathers. Wax protective amulets are sometimes made just after the full moon, as it begins to wane, to endow them with maximum protection.

However, you may prefer to work during the full moon for both power and protection. If you do create your amulet during the waning moon period, you can empower it at dawn to give it positive energies. Any time after dusk is good for creating protective amulets and they can then be left on a window ledge until dawn to absorb the rising energies.

- First choose your coloured candle. You can use more than one of different colours or a two-coloured candle to create the wax on which to etch your symbol. Beeswax is especially good since the bee, as symbol of the Mother Goddess, confers extra protection. You can buy beeswax candles dyed with vegetable dyes or undyed ones in quite deep yellows and browns.

- Place the candle directly on a fireproof tray rather than in a holder and secure it by dropping melted wax from the candle on to the tray. You can, if you wish, create circular amulets by using cake trays with large individual cups in which to stand your candle. In this way you can use different coloured candles and make several different amulets at once, perhaps one for each family member.

- Allow the candle to melt, spreading the wax so that it forms a square. Make sure it is sufficiently thick not to crack when lifted from the tray.

- As the candle burns, you may like to recite a protective chant, for example:

  Wax fall, gentle flame, wax hold this secret name.

- Repeat in your mind nine times or, if you are alone, whisper aloud the secret word of power and protection with which you will endow your amulet.

- As the wax forms, write in the air over it with your etching tool (this can be a fountain pen, an awl, a long nail or a tiny screwdriver), forming the symbols or shapes that spell out the secret word of protection and power.

- When the wax is set, ease it from the tray with a wooden spatula or knife (do this very gently).

- You can now carve a glyph, or a protective word, square pattern or a personal number charm to symbolise your secret message.

You do, of course, have the option of creating your amulet or talisman with invisible writing: you can then endow it with a complex affirmation of protection by touching the surface very lightly to leave no mark, using a pencil of the same colour as the wax.

The most magical method is to use a magic pencil: to make one, burn a stick of protective incense such as sandalwood or myrrh and then plunge it into cold water, removing it quickly before it becomes sodden. The end will now be like a pencil. If you let it dry, you can write lightly on the surface of the wax and then rub away the visible signs when it is only slightly burned.

To dedicate and empower your amulet

- Mix a few grains of salt in a dish of pure water and sprinkle a few drops around the four sides of the tablet.

- Pass the wax through the smoke of a protective incense, such as frankincense, myrrh or sandalwood.

- Finally, circle it clockwise nine times with a dark purple or blue candle. At this point you can again repeat the purpose of your amulet or talisman and the secret words of power.

Word squares

Word squares were originally created by medieval magicians, though they are attributed to ancient practitioners, or sometimes their apprentices, using corruptions of medieval Latin words. The words are written forwards, backwards, upwards and downwards. We do not know the significance of some of the letter squares, only that they have acquired power by usage over centuries. Other people use Hebrew words with great numerological significance and sometimes a pyramid formation, as with the word 'abracadabra' (see page 64).

One of the most common protective word squares was written either on parchment or wax and worn round the neck in a red flax bag, the colour and fabric being associated with the Norse Mother Goddess Frigga. You can also etch this on your wax:

```
S A T O R
A R E P O
T E N E T
O P E R A
R O T A S
```

In accordance with tradition, you should make all the letters of the same size; work from left to right, top to bottom and do not let your shadow fall on what you have etched as you work.

Sator means literally 'sower'. Arepo is 'plough', tenet means (he, she or it) 'holds'. Opera means 'work' or 'tasks' and rotas is the word for 'wheels' in the accusative or objective case. So obviously the origins of this word square are associated with the harvest and fertility. It is good for guarding against all harm and is especially potent in times of great change or uncertainty and for travellers (see also Travel and Workplace Protection, page 165).

Number charms

Numbers were also used to create talismans and amulets by applying basic numerology. Using the basic number–letter correspondences, you can make your own personalised (and secret) talismanic shapes that endow you with your own unique magical protection and power. The following table is based on the Pythagorean system of numbering letters and is most often used in numerology.

1	2	3	4	5	6	7	8	9
A	B	C	D	E	F	G	H	I
J	K	L	M	N	O	P	Q	R
S	T	U	V	W	X	Y	Z	

To create your talisman, first work out the number values of the individual letters of your name. You should use the name (both first name and surname) with which you feel most comfortable, perhaps the name that friends would use if they were sending you a birthday card or a message on the Internet. These numbers will enable you to trace out a pattern (see page 63) that forms a magic shape. You can carry this shape as a talisman.

Most of my friends would address me as Cass Eason, which would translate into this number sequence:

$$3 1 1 1 5 1 1 6 5$$

Alternatively, you can use your secret power name (see page 44).

Using magical number squares

Magic squares have been found in Jewish, Indian, Arabian and Ancient Chinese magic and are often ascribed sacred significance. In the Kabbalistic or Hebrew esoteric tradition, magical squares are called *kamea*, which means 'amulet', and were worn as pendants. The set of numbers forms a basis for marking out the numbers that correspond to the name letters. You simply trace your name on the number square to give you a personalised talismanic shape. The magic square formation shown overleaf is one of the oldest in existence.

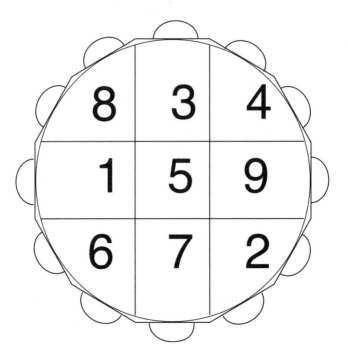

Why is this a magic square? Because, just like the magic letter square, whose letters made up the same word whether read horizontally or vertically, here the rows of numbers, whether read horizontally, vertically or diagonally, all add up to 15. The number 15 has great mystical significance. In Hebrew numerology, it is associated with the Hebrew letter *Heh*, a window that is a symbol of being able to see into other worlds. The letter has an additional meaning connected with the universal life force and so 15 is associated with life and eternity.

I have a tambourine marked with this number square which I use regularly to invoke the power inherent in the magical square and it is very reassuring if I am alone at night in the house. At different times, I tap out not only my name, but also a wish, a protective mantra or a power word.

Drawing a magic square

You can draw a magic square on absolutely anything, because it is the shape formed that is important. First mark out the numbers (see opposite for an example). Then etch the shape formed in your candle wax talisman, in parchment on paper, on a protective crystal or metal or on clay. You can even mark the shape in icing or pastry on a cake and eat it to absorb the protection quickly. Again, the shape can be transferred to a thin scroll of paper and worn in a small silver tube or locket.

If you feel under threat, you can draw your talismanic shape on a note pad at a meeting, covering it with circles or designs to keep it secret, or trace it on your hand, making your lucky talismanic shape.

Let us return to the magic number we used for my name as an example: as I explained earlier, using the number Pythagorean system of number letters, Cass Eason becomes 3 1 1 1 5 1 1 6 5.

If I trace out my sequence of numbers in a magic square, it looks like this. Note that where numbers are repeated (I have one sequence of three ones, and another of two) the line will 'zig-zag' the appropriate number of times through that number, creating a sign.

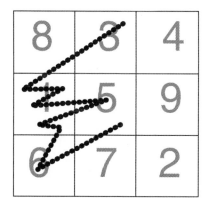 

I could trace this design and etch or draw it on an amulet.

Using a word square amulet

You can make a temporary amulet to suit a specific need for protection, such as a trip to New York, a meeting with the bank manager or critical ex-partner. Write out the numbers of a word or phrase that sums up your need. For example if you were nervous of flying you might write:

Safe Plane

1165 73155

You would then trace out the design, as shown overleaf, remembering to zig-zag back if a letter is repeated, and etch or draw it on an amulet, and carry it with you for extra protection during the particular event.

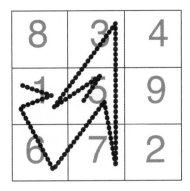

Once you have used your temporary amulet, thank the benign forces who have protected you. If your amulet is biodegradable or made from a natural substance such as crystal or pure metal, bury it in a secret place and plant seeds on top. If it is not, dispose of it in an environmentally friendly way: cover it with salt and seal it in a brown paper bag, tied with nine tight knots of red twine and place it at the bottom of a bin or rubbish heap.

Abracadabra

The word 'abracadabra' is usually associated with conjuring tricks such as when a magician produces a rabbit out of a hat. In earlier times, however, it was considered a powerful talisman, used by the Roman Gnostics, a group who claimed to have esoteric mystical knowledge, for invoking the aid of good spirits as protection against disease, misfortune and death.

Sammonicus, a Gnostic physician, used the magical triangle for curing agues and fevers, especially those that were long-lasting. He said that the letters should be written on paper, folded into the shape of a cross, and worn

ABRACADABRA
BRACADABR
RACADAB
ACADA
CAD
A

ABRACADABRA
ABRACADABR
ABRACADAB
ABRACADA
ABRACAD
ABRACA
ABRAC
ABRA
ABR
AB
A

for nine days suspended from the neck. On the tenth day, before sunrise, it was to be cast behind the patient into a stream running eastward.

The Abracadabra charm remained popular and was used in Europe during the Middle Ages. It was also sold as a talisman, often wreathed with lavender, during the Great Plague of London in 1665, to offer protection against infection.

The nature of its protection depends on how it is created. It can be either a short-lived protection, written on paper and afterwards burned or thrown away, or a more elaborate piece of paper in a tube or locket or in a small charm bag around your neck or waist. It is not a charm to etch on a crystal where the letters can be seen, not least because you will have to explain to curious, and sometimes sceptical, acquaintances your apparent interest in conjuring tricks.

Using a temporary Abracadabra to banish negative energy

This ritual aims to use the Abracadabra formula to banish danger, depression or anxiety from your life, alleviate a chronic physical condition or to banish a destructive habit, lingering doubts or regrets.

- Write one of the two forms of Abracadabra shown on page 64 on a triangle of white paper, using red ink.

- Fold it and place inside a small dark purse of leather or natural fabric. Carry it during the day and place it beside your bed at night for nine days and nights.

- At dusk on the tenth day, unfold the paper and recite the charm, beginning with the full word and working downwards towards a single A, decreasing the syllables until there are no more letters left, and leaving a gap for the silence when the final A has been spoken.

- Repeat this nine times and then hold the paper under water until the ink runs and the paper disintegrates. If you prefer, you can follow the older tradition of casting the paper over your shoulder into an eastward-flowing stream.

Once you have completed the ritual, the problem or illness should then fade. If it does not, continue to repeat the charm.

A permanent Abracadabra charm for safety

This ritual shows you how to make a permanent empowering Abracadabra charm for keeping you safe, preserving good health and increasing good fortune. An Abracadabra power charm works on the reverse principle. It is a cumulative protective and health-preserver and so should be recited nine times, beginning with the single A sound and ending with the full word 'abracadabra'.

- Take small triangular piece of paper, parchment, clay or wax.

- Beginning at the bottom, paint or etch the single letter, then continue writing the charm, going upwards and working from left to right, until the full word is at the top.

- Place the charm by your bed to attract health-giving powers and good luck while you sleep. It will also protect against bad dreams.

- Alternatively, carve an equilateral triangle of wood with a hole bored in it at the top and paint the charm on it.

- Pass a leather thong through the hole and recite the Abracadabra charm, starting with A and ending with the full word. Repeat it nine times, before placing the charm around your neck, so that the charm faces your neck and cannot be seen. You can paint your zodiacal glyph or a lucky symbol on the visible side.

- At bedtime and in the morning, recite the sounds nine times.

You can, if you prefer, place it inside a small charm bag on a piece of cord to hang around your neck or waist or keep it in your bag or pocket.

Empowering your Acabradabra charm

The charm should have sufficient power within it not to need recharging. However, if you are facing particular stress or sense the onset of a chronic condition, use the following ritual to imbue it with extra power.

- Light a golden candle for the power of the Sun and a silver candle for the power of the Moon and place them on either side of your charm or pendant when you take it off at night.

- Sprinkle a circle of salt round the charm and candles, and place a few drops of peppermint oil or essence on a dish next to the charm for protection.

- Before you go to sleep, blow out the candles encircling the charm and yourself with protective light.

FIVE

Psychic Protection in Nature

All around us the natural world offers, in flowers, trees and herbs, gentle yet potent means of protection that have been part of the lives of men and women for countless centuries for banishing and keeping away negativity. Used in times past to repel supernatural forces that were blamed for bad harvests, storms or sickness among animals, these natural substances are filled with the life force, or *prana*, as it is sometimes called. In the modern world, they also protect against pollution and the stresses of modern living as well as against more deliberate malevolence.

Trees as a source of protection

Trees are said to link the Earth with the sky and so have been regarded as protective for thousands of years. Nyd, or Need, fires – the holy fires of the Teutonic and Celtic peoples – were burned at the spring equinox or Beltane (May Eve) from nine different kinds of wood. Sticks were rubbed together or a more elaborate oaken spindle was turned in an oaken log-socket to kindle flames, and from this central fire all other fires and church candles at Easter were lit. Charred sticks from these fires were kept to protect the home from fire, storm and flood. In Scandinavia, a Midsummer Tree is still built in gardens and meadows on Midsummer Day from leafy branches and is the focus of communal dancing and singing.

A *protective tree spell to remove negative feelings*

Traditionally a hazel, an oak, an elm and a willow twig had to be found for this spell but in practice it works well with any four different woods. There are many variations of this spell. I discovered this version only recently and it seems very effective.

- Collect four twigs from four different woods.

- Make a fire, out of doors if possible, and hold each wood in the smoke, turning it nine times anti-clockwise as you repeat these words:

> *Turner be turned,*
> *Burner be burned,*
> *Let only good*
> *Come of this wood.*

- Then endow each twig with a bad feeling or experience and cast it on the fire, repeating:

> *Turner be turned,*
> *Burner be burned,*
> *Bad times destroy,*
> *Leave only joy.*

- When the fire is burned through, the bad feelings will be gone.

- To finish the ritual, wait until the fire has completely gone out, then scoop a handful of cold ashes and bury them beneath a living tree, saying:

> *Ashes to ashes,*
> *Buried and gone,*
> *Old sorrows ended,*
> *New growth begun.*

- Scatter a few seeds to grow beneath the tree, or plant an acorn or fruit stone in a barren place.

Protective trees

Some people believe that deforestation is an underlying cause of the increased violence and crime the world suffers today, as well as causing environmental harm. This underlines the protective forces that trees have in nature. The hawthorn and rowan trees are species traditionally associated with protecting homes and their occupants, as well as outbuildings and animals, but many trees do naturally repel harm and absorb malevolence, converting it into new life.

Many countries, including the UK, are reintroducing native species and there is a welcome revival of local woodcarving. As a result, you can buy a variety of artefacts made of different woods. Alternatively, you may like to visit an arboretum where there is a great variety of trees and obtain your own fallen or dead branches, which you can rub smooth and fashion with a knife into different forms to remind you of the specific qualities of each different kind of wood. For example, some people make tiny crescent moon shapes out of willow, as this is the tree associated with lunar goddesses.

You can also create your personal power animal (see page 42) from an appropriate wood. Endow your statue with protection by reciting a mantra as you work, such as:

Guardian tree, protecting me, watch me while I work and sleep.
From my path all danger keep;
Let me only be surrounded by tranquillity.

These old rhymes were the way our ancestors transmitted the natural lore that was a part of every household and which was passed down orally from generation to generation. What they lacked in sophistication, they made up for in the accumulated hopes and faith of their simpler world.

Ash

The ash, known as a father tree, offers a safe passage to travellers, especially on sea journeys and those who settle in other countries. It was a holy tree to the Celts and as late as the nineteenth century, in Killura in Ireland, a descendant of the original sacred ash of Creevna was used as a charm against drowning. After the potato famine in Ireland, emigrants took the tree with them to America to guard them from harm.

Bamboo

This protects household boundaries from burglars and intrusive visitors and repels psychic attack.

Birch

The birch is a tree of purification, symbolic of the rebirth of spring, and is a tree associated with the Mother Goddess. On the religious festival of Whitsun, in remote parts of Russia, traces of this older form of worship remain as birch trees are dressed in women's clothes to represent the coming of the summer. Throughout Europe, birch twigs are still used in rituals to expel evil spirits in ancient ceremonies such as beating the bounds or marking out territories, and they appear in New Year celebrations throughout the northern hemisphere to drive out the spirits of the old year. Birch cradles were carved to protect babies and the very young.

Blackthorn

Because it blooms when the bitter north-east winds are at their height, the protection of the blackthorn comes into its own when life is really hard.

The blackthorn produces white blossoms on an almost black branch and is said to bloom at midnight on Christmas Eve. This imbues it with a holy significance which counters the often unfairly negative perceptions of the thorn. It will form a barrier against both physical and psychic attack, and planted in a garden will tangle up all harshness and spite that might otherwise enter the home.

Coconut

A mother tree, the coconut offers protection, especially to mothers and children, and absorbs potential cruelty and aggression. The fruit forms a fertility symbol and so the tree also guards against those who would drain inspiration and joy.

Elder

A tree of the White (Moon) Goddess of the Celts, this tree is said to belong to all female gods whose protection extends to the home and family. Known as a fairy tree, elder absorbs personal and spirit negativity and is said to strengthen intuition and clairvoyance, and so is a good tree to use for protection in during divinatory or psychic work.

Hawthorn

The hawthorn is sacred to Mars and also to Thor and other Northern gods of thunder. It is believed to act as a shield against physical and psychic harm. In pre-Christian times, it was planted around sacred boundaries and many white witches traditionally surrounded their homes with hawthorns to keep out prying eyes. The expression 'haw witch' (*haw* is old English for 'hedge'), used to describe a solitary practitioner of magic, exists on both sides of the Atlantic. A hawthorn amulet is still powerful against intrusion and idle gossip.

The hawthorn is a fairy tree and its protection is increased at magical times such as May Day (1 May), Midsummer Eve (20 or 21 June) or Hallowe'en (31 October). On these days, it is said that if you sit beneath the hawthorn you will be enchanted by the little people.

A hawthorn or hazel rod, made by stripping the bark and smoothing the wood, sometimes engraved with the shape of a woodland creature or caduceus (see page 49), forms a good protective charm.

Hazel

Traditionally a tree of wisdom and justice, the hazel marks boundaries against unjust treatment. Hazel rods were taken by Irish settlers to America to keep away snakes. It also is said that a charred hazel twig from one of the festival fires burned on Easter or May Eve, kept in the family hearth, will offer protection against storms and household disasters.

Holly

King of the waning year, its name means 'holy', and so holly is clearly associated with spirituality. Hung as a wreath on the door, it will offer protection to dispossessed tree spirits who will thereby bring good fortune and prosperity to the home and its occupants.

Juniper

A tree whose berries are associated with New Year purification of stale energies, the juniper offers protection against all forms of malevolence and drives away bad luck.

Larch

Larch offers protection against thieves and all those who would do you personal harm; it also restores optimism.

Laurel

Laurel guards against illness and failure, especially in career, and offers the strength to win through in spite of difficulty.

Pine

A symbol of fire and illumination, pine is associated with the cleansing fire that purges away what is redundant or destructive. Pine was used in the resin torches that lit the halls throughout Northern Europe before the days of gas and electric light, and so it has become associated with the torch that flames in the darkness.

In the Isles of Orkney, until the beginning of the twentieth century, it was the custom to whirl a flaming pine torch around the heads of a mother and her newly delivered child to purify them.

Rowan or mountain ash

This tree is sacred to the Moon, protecting households from harm, and is the tree of happy homes. Traditionally, a rowan twig was removed from a tree, using the hands, not a knife, then fastened in the shape of a cross with red twine and used as a protective device for stables, cowsheds and outbuildings to guard against bad witches, spirits, mischievous fairies and all enchantment. The cross-beams of chimneys in old cottages were sometimes constructed of rowan, and a rowan twig tied to a cow's tail was said to prevent bad witches stealing or souring milk. The milk was also churned in a vessel made of rowan to prevent enchantment.

Rowan was regarded as powerful against all malice, malevolence and illusion, but the crosses of rowan combined with birch that were put over doorways at dawn on May morning for year-round protection were replaced each year. In the same way, in accordance with this early practice, rowan amulets should be replaced every May morning.

Willow
The willow, another tree sacred to the Moon Goddesses, offers protection to people and their homes, and leaves or branches are hung in the home for this purpose. It also frees blocked emotions.

Herbs as a source of protection

There are many ways of using herbs as a form of protection. When their positive qualities are absorbed – through burning them as incense or oils, or using them for bathing, or eating or drinking certain culinary herbs as an infusion or tea – their healing and restorative properties can offer immediate as well as long-term benefits. For a more gradual cumulative effect, herbs have traditionally been carried in sachets or small bags, made into pot pourri, hung in bunches around the home or planted in pots in the home or workplace to offer a shield against harm. Later in this chapter I have listed different uses for protective herbs.

If you are using herbs in baths or teas, you should be aware that herbs are not without side effects, especially if taken over a long period or in large quantities. **Some should not be taken if you are pregnant or suffer from certain medical conditions.**

Herbs that should **not** be used during pregnancy include: anise, angelica, autumn crocus, barberry, basil, bay, cedarwood, clary sage, elderflower (also not suitable for nursing mothers), fennel, golden seal, juniper, male fern, mandrake, marjoram, myrrh, parsley, pennyroyal, poke root, rue, sage, southernwood, tansy, tarragon, thuja, thyme, wintergreen, worm-wood and yarrow. My best advice is to consult your doctor or midwife before using any herbs if you are pregnant, especially in the first three months.

Always use a reliable commercial product and check the label. If in doubt, consult a reliable herbal book (see Further Reading, page 179) or ask a herbalist or pharmacist.

Herbal baths

Herbal baths have been used in many different times and traditions, and before the days of plumbed-in hot water, the bath was taken in a tub using pure running water, collected from a stream, the sea or rainwater that had not touched the ground. The water would be heated in huge copper pots over a fire. Natural pools were also adapted as baths in country places and purifying herbs added to the water. These herbal soaks offered protection while travelling, before battle, before childbirth and at all times when danger, malevolence or illness were near.

Water would be poured over the head as part of ritual cleaning, usually seven or nine times, and a magical phrase chanted, such as:

> I wash away all cares,
> I wash away all sorrows,
> I wash away all hostility.

A baby would be bathed in water that had been run over an iron sickle to endow the water with the protection of iron (see Protective Crystals and Metals, page 87) and a gentle herb such a chamomile added to protect the infant from the dangers of early life.

Herbal baths at night are still a way of removing the stresses of the day, and in the early morning of absorbing protection; many of the modern herbal bath preparations were first used thousands of years ago for similar purposes. For example, hyssop is mentioned in the Bible as a spiritually cleansing herb. It is just as magical to use a ready-prepared herbal mix in the bath as it is to use fresh herbs (and rather less messy if you are in a hurry). Herbs that are safe to take as infusions or teas are usually also safe in baths, unless you have allergies or sensitive skin.

Traditionally fresh herbs were chopped and added to the tin tub by the fire, but modern plumbing means that you cannot add fresh or dried herbs directly to the bath water without risking clogging up the pipes. A better method is to place a handful of herbs in a bag of muslin, cheesecloth or similar material in the bath, as the water runs, so the herbal fragrance will infuse the water. This was the method employed by our more fastidious ancestors who preferred not to end up with pieces sticking to their skin.

Making a herbal bath

- Make a bag from a rectangle of muslin (cheesecloth) about 12 x 20 cm/4½ x 8 in. Fold the cloth in half to make a square pocket, stitch the sides and fill with herbs.

- Tie the bag with string or cord in a natural fabric in a colour that will not run when wet.

- Run your bath, then place the bag of herbs in the water for ten minutes. Remove the bag before you bathe, squeezing out any remaining liquid from the herbs.

- Alternatively, hang the bag just below the hot tap and let the water run through it as you fill the bath.

For speed, you can also use a knotted stocking or a leg cut from a pair of sheer tights to hold your herbs.

If you prefer, instead of adding the herbs to the bath water, you can make a strong herbal infusion by mixing half a cup of herbs with 1.2 litres/2 pints/ 5 cups of boiling water, and add that instead.

- Steep for about 20 minutes, strain the liquid and add it to the bath water. As you soak in the water, visualise the tension and negativity flowing away and energy or tranquillity replacing them.

Herbal baths for protective and restorative energies

Combine two or three of each of the following herbs in your herbal bag. You can also experiment with mixes of your own, although you may wish to begin by using commercially prepared products and seeing which herbs suit you. You can add to the effects by varying the temperature of the bath water. Warm baths are soothing and cooler water is stimulating. Use only pure herbs. If you are using fresh herbs, gather only from unpolluted sources – grow them in your garden or buy them from a reputable garden shop or herbalist – and rinse before using.

Experiment with small quantities. If you do have sensitive skin, make weak infusions and experiment with small quantities of individual herbs. For babies and children, use only delicate herbs such as chamomile, rose and lavender. Probably with babies and very young children I would begin with a commercial, chemical-free ready-made mixture that is tested as safe for little ones. Once again, remember to exercise great caution when taking herbal baths if you are pregnant.

Before a herbal bath, burn protective purple, pink or deep blue candles in the evening and white or pink in the early morning. Alternatively, bathe in the natural morning light or the rays of the setting sun.

To attract positive energies at the beginning of a new day: Comfrey, dandelion leaves, hips, lavender, mint (use a small amount only as it can be an irritant), orange blossom or peel, raspberry leaves, rose petals or sandalwood.

To soothe away tensions and encourage quiet contemplation: Chamomile flowers, elder flowers, elecampane, lemon balm (use sparingly), valerian roots, vervain and violet petals (violet can sometimes cause nausea in pregnancy).

To remove feelings of irritability and frustration and promote acceptance of what cannot be changed: Calendula (marigold), elecampane, evening primrose, honeysuckle, lavender, linden flowers, marsh mallow, myrtle, rose petals and tansy.

To protect yourself from intrusion into your personal space: Catnip, geranium petals, jasmine flowers, orange flowers, rosemary, thyme and vetivert roots.

For protection if you have been or are surrounded by negativity or hostility: Angelica root, anise, apple blossom, basil, bay, cloves, juniper berries, elder flowers, lavender, patchouli, pine needles, sage, raspberry leaves and lime blossoms.

To banish negative influences and destructive habits: Calendula (marigold), chamomile, cloves, eucalyptus leaves, lavender, lemon rind (use sparingly), marjoram, meadowsweet and valerian.

For clearing indecision when people are pressurising or bombarding you with conflicting opinions: Elder flowers, lemon verbena, lovage, mint, nettle, pennyroyal, pine needles, sage, savory and thyme.

For repelling malevolence and psychic or psychological attack: Cinnamon (sparingly), comfrey, dill, eucalyptus, pine needles, rose hips, rose petals, sweet fennel, vervain.

To protect yourself before divination or psychic work: Anise, bay, jasmine, lavender, orange, sandalwood.

Fragrant herbs

You may wish to include a herb that will make your bath aromatic. The traditional herbal recipes of our ancestors often used rather unpleasant-smelling herbs to drive away what they believed were evil spirits, but friends and work colleagues may be less tolerant! The following herbs are especially fragrant:

Angelica, apple blossom, bay, chamomile flowers, cloves, geranium, jasmine, honeysuckle, lavender, lemon, lime blossoms, lovage, mint, myrtle, orange, patchouli, pennyroyal, rose petals, rosemary, sandalwood.

Oats offer gentle protection and can be added to any bath. Soak the oatmeal in warm water in a non-porous cloth, for example a sock tied at the top, then squeeze out the liquid into the bath.

The magic of herbs

Herbs are potent in psychic protection since each herb also has empowering or luck-bringing properties that replace the tensions or negativity removed or repelled by the herb. The botanical names are given in brackets. You can build up a collection of potted herbs in the home, grow them in the garden or use them in pot pourri or sachets, as well as burning them.

Agrimony (Agrimonia eupatoria)

Agrimony will banish negative energies and return them to the sender and is often used in herbal protection sachets for this reason; prevents nightmares and insomnia, especially when you are over-tired; may be added to a sleep pillow.

Ruled by Jupiter.

Aloe (Aloe vera)

A protective plant, if grown in pots in the house; in the kitchen its presence is said to prevent burns and accidents; brings luck and prosperity.

Ruled by the Moon.

Althea (Althea officinalis)

Protects against negativity in others and from unknown forces; helps communication with angelic/spirit guides.

Ruled by the Moon.

Alyssum (Alyssum)

Protects from anger of others and self-destructive anger; traditionally hung in the home to prevent others seducing partners and lovers. A potted version for the office can deter workplace flirtations.

Ruled by Venus.

Anemone (Anemone pulsatilla)

Protects against illness; traditionally used in a red healing bag with other healing herbs to keep away infection.

Ruled by Mars.

Angelica (Angelica archangelica)

Keeps away illness and hostility of all kinds. It is especially protective for children; can also be worn as an amulet in a herb sachet, or used as a defensive shield when grown in domestic boundaries or window boxes and kitchen pots. Brings luck, especially in speculation.

Ruled by the Sun.

Anise/Aniseed *(Pimpinella anisum)*
A potent cleanser of negativity, especially at home, and a natural protector burned as incense before psychic work; another ingredient for a sleep pillow as anise guards against bad dreams. A preserver of youth.

Ruled by Jupiter.

Balm of Gilead *(Commiphora opobalsamum)*
Protective, especially of lovers; heals feelings after betrayals and sorrow, bringing new love and keeping it true.

Ruled by Venus.

Bistort *(Polygonum bistorta)*
Bistort is said to be protective against spirit attack and hauntings in the home, when burned or sprinkled around the home as an infusion. Kept near the doorway, it will prevent unwelcome visitors; excellent for diverting uninvited salespersons; good for prosperity, fertility and increasing psychic awareness.

Ruled by Saturn.

Bladderwrack *(Fucus visiculosus)*
Protective for travellers or sailors on the sea or those who travel abroad; guards the bearer against accidents; a money-bringer.

Ruled by the Moon.

Borage *(Borago officinalis)*
A herb of courage, especially when the flowers are carried or worn; carried in a sachet will provide safety for all outdoor activities and in potentially hazardous places; increases psychic awareness as well as courage.

Ruled by Jupiter.

Buckthorn *(Rhammus)*
Deters unfriendly paranormal presences; fights against injustice in matters of law and officialdom; good for granting wishes.

Ruled by Saturn.

Burdock *(Arctium lappa)*

Protects against negativity in the home when burned as incense and used in sachets or pot pourri; a powerful personal amulet and luck-bringer if gathered during the waning moon and tied with nine knots of red wool or thin twine.

Ruled by Venus.

Caraway *(Carum carvi)*

Seeds hidden in personal possessions when they must be left unattended will deter thieves. Keep a small sachet hidden in the car or in computer cases; attracts love.

Ruled by Mercury.

Cayenne pepper *(Capiscum animum)*

Like salt, pepper traditionally offers domestic protection, whether added to a floor wash or scattered around a room; deters hostile visitors and dispels lingering depression; returns bad vibes to the sender; induces love and passion.

Ruled by Mars.

Celandine *(Chelidonium majus)*

Offers relief from sorrows or difficulties; lessens the hold of addictions, obsessions, false friends or unwise offers of instant wealth or success; also offers protection against false accusations; a herb of happiness that enhances powers of persuasion.

Ruled by the Sun.

Chamomile *(Anthemis nobilis)*

A protective herb; can be scattered around boundary fences or house entrances to deter unwelcome and unfriendly visitors; especially protective towards children; a curse-breaker. Brings kindness and gentleness.

Ruled by the Sun.

Clover *(Trifolium extraction)*

All clover is protective against external attack, especially during travelling and despair; protects against bad luck; also attracts love, money and good fortune.

Ruled by Mercury.

Cloves *(Syzygium aromaticum)*

Cloves, kept in a protective sachet or carried as an amulet, or burned as incense, deter gossip, malice and envy against the wearer and will soften the pain of sorrow after loss; potent against psychic attack; increases concentration and mental acuity.

Ruled by Jupiter.

Comfrey *(Symphytum officinale)*

A herb for safe travel; hidden in a sachet in a suitcase, comfrey guards possessions belongings from loss or theft; a natural luck- and money-bringer.

Ruled by Saturn.

Dill *(Anethum graveolens)*

One of the traditional protective herbs. In the home, fresh dill tied with red twine can be hung from the ceiling next to the doorway to keep away all who would speak or do harm: it should be regularly replaced. The dried seed heads can be placed above cradles to protect infants, or scattered around the boundaries of a home especially at midsummer. Attracts money and passion.

Ruled by Mercury.

Dragon's blood *(Daemonorops draco)*

Used mainly as a protective incense, it can also be powdered and sprinkled on door frames and window sills, to prevent negativity entering your home. In a sachet, gives one a low profile in potentially dangerous or confrontational situations; good for protecting against potential violence; increases male potency and empowers both men and women.

Ruled by Mars.

Elder *(Sambucus nigra)*

One of the most protective herbs in magic; folklore promises that by scattering elder leaves to the four winds and over your head, your free will is reactivated if people or circumstances have been influencing you unduly or misleading you; elder flowers strengthen the innate power to fight compulsions; elder twigs in the home guard against storm damage; berries beneath the pillow will banish insomnia and bring good dreams to the sleeper; promises prosperity, happy marriage and fertility.

Ruled by Venus.

Elecampane *(Inula helenium)*
Known also as elfwort, so associated with elves and fairies; protective when burned before divination or psychic work; also enhances positive psychic awareness and acts as a love charm.

Ruled by Jupiter.

Fennel *(Foeniculum vulgare var dulce)*
Grown in the garden or hung in windows, offers protection from unwanted visitors and malevolence; especially guards children against tension; traditionally replaced every Midsummer Eve, fennel brings courage.

Ruled by Mercury.

Garlic *(Allium sativum)*
Said to offer protection against vampires and werewolves; will banish any form of negativity, earthly or otherwise. A string of garlic bulbs hung in the kitchen will absorb any irritations and bad temper; this should be replaced regularly and the old cloves buried. The string formation is especially potent and in a new home this can drive away any ghosts or negativity lingering from the previous owners; attracts prosperity and good health.

Ruled by Mars.

Honesty *(Lunaria extraction)*
Dried honesty, once a feature in many homes, will drive away all fears of the dark in adults or children; attracts money.

Ruled by the Moon.

Hops *(Humulus lupulus)*
Used in healing incenses and sachets, since they drive away all dark thoughts, doubts and fears. Hop pillows are a traditional remedy for insomnia and bring happy dreams, although they are not pleasant-smelling (except to lovers of ale).

Ruled by Mars.

Hyssop *(Hyssopus officinalis)*
Primarily a herb of purification, used in magical rituals to cleanse magical tools and in the home to dispel doubts and fears. A few drops of hyssop infusion is useful to sprinkle over inherited artefacts with sad memories and any newly acquired items from car boot or garage sales whose history you do not know.

Ruled by Jupiter.

Knotweed *(Polygonum aviculare)*

As its name suggests, in plant form this is good grown near the front or back doors or in pots on window ledges to bind others and prevent them from doing ill; you can also banish sorrows, fears and destructive habits by naming one for each piece of herb and then casting it into running water; ensures fidelity.

Ruled by Saturn.

Lavender *(Lavendula)*

Can be used for absolutely any protective purpose; gentle, deters harsh words or actions especially in relationships; brings quiet sleep and peace of mind by banishing fears of all kinds; protects children and babies and anyone who is sick or vulnerable; brings reconciliation.

Ruled by Mercury.

Lemongrass *(Cymbopogon citratus)*

Repels spite and gossip; good to burn before family gatherings; protects also against snakes, both reptilian and human, who seek to deceive; lessens the power of obsessions and destructive relationships; increases intuitive powers.

Ruled by Mercury.

Lucky hand root *(Orchis extraction)*

A well-known magical herb for safe travel and to prevent redundancy and job loss; conveys protection while travelling and safety from con-merchants; used in magic bags (see page 37); actively attracts good fortune, money-making (traditionally carried by gamblers) and career opportunities. Not for internal use.

Ruled by Venus.

Mugwort *(Artemisia vulgaris)*

Used for protection in all forms of divination and to colour water for candle scrying; traditionally believed to repel all earthly and other-worldly malevolence when hung in entrances; brings strength and increases psychic awareness.

Ruled by Venus.

Mullein *(Verbascum tharpus)*

Another cleansing herb that repels all negativity and gives courage; traditionally protects from psychic attacks and from demons (e.g. depression and self-doubt) within as well as beyond the mind; leaves are carried as amulets by travellers to prevent accidents, especially in remote places. Another sleep pillow ingredient, mullein protects against nightmares and negativity that may float your way during the night. Used in formal magical rituals and psychic work to offer protection and awaken divinatory powers.

Ruled by Saturn.

Myrrh *(Commiphora myrrha)*
A purifying and healing herb, often burned as incense along with empowering frankincense in formal magic and to cleanse ritual objects before use. Brings healing and spirituality to areas of the home and workplace in which it has been burned as oil or incense; increasingly used as a domestic incense for banishing fears; good for meditation and visualisation; strengthens the natural protective aura we all possess.

Ruled by the Moon.

Nettle *(Urtica dioica)*
Nettle is a defensive herb and so is important in psychic self-defence as well as protecting the boundaries of a home. Some people deliberately leave a nettle patch close to a boundary fence, away from children's reach, to form a natural protective barrier against all harm, including intruders, malevolence and unwelcome visitors, earthly and otherwise; freshly cut nettles, placed in a pot beneath the bed, are believed to drive away any sickness; a herb of courage when facing and overcoming difficulty.

Ruled by Mars.

Parsley *(Petroselinum sativum)*
A herb of purification; hung in the home or growing in pots, parsley is protective against all negativity; traditionally it should be planted on Good Friday, the day on which evil is said to have no power; attracts money and passion.

Ruled by Mercury.

Pennyroyal *(Mentha pulegium)*
A herb said in times past to offer protection against the evil eye and curses; potent in repelling all malevolence, both earthly and paranormal; kept in the home, it prevents quarrels especially between lovers and can also be carried in small fabric sachets as an amulet of peace.

Ruled by Mars.

Peppermint *(Mentha piperita)*

A healing and purifying herb, burned as incense at home or in sickrooms and used as a floor wash to drive away all negativity and illness; in the bathroom, the oil and infusion placed around plug holes will prevent the re-entry of redundant energies; another ingredient in sleep pillows to keep away bad dreams and night phantoms.

Ruled by Mercury.

Rose *(Rosa extraction)*

A bringer of harmony when burned or used in sachets; keeps away anger and transforms sorrow to joy, hatred to gentleness, cruelty to kindness; excellent for children who are having a bad time with bullying or feel misunderstood; also brings luck in financial matters.

Ruled by Venus.

Rosemary *(Rosemarinus officinalis)*

Perhaps the most common herb of purification, used in protective bottles and charms, and burned as incense or oil in informal and ceremonial magic; drives away all kinds of negativity and illness and repels thieves and vandals from the home, whether the fresh herb is hung up or used dried in pot pourri; in the bedroom, rosemary prevents bad dreams. Increases concentration and improves memory; enhances prophetic and divinatory abilities, love and passion.

Ruled by the Sun.

Rue *(Ruta graveolens)*

Associated with regrets and another traditional defence against the evil eye, rue is a powerful protector against all malevolence or curses, returning any ill wishes or bad charms to the sender; a good general household purifier; brings healing and good health.

Ruled by Mars.

Sage *(Salvia officinalis)*

The herb of long life and wisdom; said to offer protection against the evil eye and curses; when burned as incense or oil, sage guards the home and family. Traditionally the herb should be thrown on an open fire, whilst the words 'Sorrows away' are said nine times; enhances divinatory powers and brings health and money.

Ruled by Jupiter.

Sandalwood (Santalum album)

Protective, especially when burned as incense or oil; drives away negative energies in the home; is used in ceremonial magic to provide psychic protection; also offers domestic and personal security and can be used as an amulet; said to make contact with guardian angels and the Higher Self easier and to enhance magical abilities.

Ruled by Jupiter.

Thistle (Carduus extraction)

Like nettle, thistle forms a natural psychic as well as physical barrier to negativity; offers protection against thieves, lingering sadness and active hostility or spite in thought or deed by enemies and those who are jealous; speeds up healing.

Ruled by Mars.

Thistle, holy (Centauria benedicta)

Known as the blessed thistle, this was used as a herb of exorcism and as a protection against evil and evil influences, both earthly and paranormal; good for banishing fears when alone or in the dark, it is also an aid to any spiritual work and contact with the Higher Self or guardian angels; encourages altruism.

Ruled by Mars.

Thyme (Thymus vulgaris)

Used for purification in both formal and informal magical rituals and as a way of banishing sorrows or regrets from the past; prevents nightmares but encourages prophetic dreams; increases psychic powers; improves memory; good for love spells and divination.

Ruled by Venus.

Valerian (Valeriana officinalis)

Protects against external hostility, inner fears and despair. Used as a herb of reconciliation: the herb is placed in dolls, which who are then tied together to bring harmony to a relationship or reunite those parted by anger or circumstance; another ingredient of sleep pillows.

Ruled by Venus.

Vervain (Verbena officinalis)

Vervain offers protection against all negativity, both earthly and spirit, and is said to have the power to turn enemies into friends if you wear it as an amulet; it also guards against lies and deceit in others, and against nightmares; good for seeing the future and for promoting fidelity in love.

Ruled by Venus.

Vetivert *(Vetiveria zizanioides)*

Breaks a run of bad luck, and prevents money draining away from you, either through trickery or hard luck stories; deflects curses and malevolence and drives away psychic attackers.

Ruled by Venus.

Witch hazel *(Hamamelis virginiana)*

As an amulet, witch hazel heals the pains of unrequited or faithless love and helps weaken destructive influences; helps to find what is lost.

Ruled by the Sun.

Making magical herb sachets

From time immemorial, herbs have been carried in tiny sachets, purses or bags to offer protection as well as to bring love, prosperity and healing and as pillows to bring peaceful sleep. They can also be placed in drawers to bring protection to different rooms or the workplace. Sometimes a tiny protective crystal, such as rose quartz or amethyst is added (see Protective Crystals and Metals, page 87).

Though herb sachets are available commercially, you can quite easily make your own, using dried herbs purchased from a supermarket or herbalist and dried flower petals or crushed tree bark. (You can prepare this yourself or buy it as part of a pot pourri mix.)

- On a bright, sunny day, mix all the herbs in a ceramic, glass or wooden bowl and run your fingers through them, naming each herb and its quality and filling it with light. For example,

   Lavender of light, lavender of love, protect me from
   harsh words and cruel deeds.

- Use a square of natural fabric such as felt, wool or cotton about 10–25 cm/4–10 in, depending on whether you want to wear or carry the sachet or use it in the home. Alternatively, you can purchase or make a tiny drawstring bag or fabric purse for the herbs.

- Place about 15 ml/1 tbsp of dried, ground herbs – you can use a single herb or a mixture of two or three – in the centre of the cloth, using more for a larger sachet.

- Tie the material in three consecutive knots of a natural twine (traditionally this should be red or purple), saying as you do so:

> *Knot one, protect me from harm inflicted by others;*
> *whether intentional or misdirected malevolence.*
> *Knot two, guard me from my own negativity, weakness and fears*
> *that are magnified by the night.*
> *Knot three, protect me with the power of light and love*
> *and grant me peaceful sleep and joy when I wake*
> *to fulfil the promise of each new day.*

- If your herbs are not very fragrant, you can add a few drops of a protective essential oil such as geranium, lavender, lemon, mint, rose or ylang-ylang.

Carry the sachet until it loses its fragrance unless it is for short-term protection, perhaps for a specific journey.

When you wish to replace the herbs, open the sachet and scatter some of the herbs to the four winds, burn a few, bury some and dissolve the rest in water. Replace the herbs by empowering new ones.

SIX

Protective Crystals
and Metals

Protective crystals

All crystals have natural protective powers since they come from the Earth and have been formed by the interaction of volcanic Fire, Water and Air over thousands of years, so absorbing the protection as well as the power inherent in the ancient elements. Many people regard crystal energies as a living force, and certainly few who hold crystals fail to experience the energising or calming influences that seem to strengthen the human auric force field – and it is true that animals and plants will also instantly gain vitality when healed with crystals.

Over the centuries, some crystals have become particularly associated with protection, exuding calming and healing energies and replacing negativity with love and optimism. Protective crystals have been recognised by many ancient peoples including the Ancient Egyptians, and traditionally include: amethyst, black agate, bloodstone, carnelian, garnet, black and red jasper, lapis lazuli, tiger's eye, topaz and turquoise. However, you may discover another crystal or even a stone from the seashore that fills you with calm and confidence; you can carry or hold this at times when you feel vulnerable and you will find that it increases in power the more you use it.

Build up a collection of small protective crystals with which you can ring your bed for quiet sleep, or place around your home or workplace to absorb the negativity of others. Buy or make a dark silk or natural fabric drawstring bag in which you can carry a protective crystal whenever you leave home.

Cleansing crystals and gemstones

When you obtain a new crystal, you should cleanse it before charging it with your own personal energies. In this way you can remove all the energies (not necessarily negative) of those who have prepared, packed and sold the stone. However, if the stone was a gift, you may wish to accept the loving energies with which it was offered and rely on your innate defensive powers to filter out any unconscious negativity, left from the previous owner's life.

Crystals should also be cleansed regularly both before and after use. Protective crystals should be washed in running water after psychic and healing work and at regular intervals even when they are not in use. If you have been in touch with a particularly negative influence, wash the stones and sprinkle them with salt. Then pass over them an incense stick or oil burner with a fragrance such as lavender, pine or rose and a candle flame of purple, silver or pink, for the healing power of the other three elements Earth, Air and Fire.

Once the crystals have dried naturally in the light of the sun, moon or stars, wrap them for a few days in a dark cloth, to restore connection with the gentle protection of the earth and to let them rest to grow strong.

Cleansing using the forces of nature

The process here is very simple: leave the crystal in sunlight and moonlight for a 24-hour period, or in a rainstorm. Alternatively, bury the crystal in a pot of herbs, for example lavender, sage or rosemary. Leave it for 24 hours and then, if necessary, wash off any remaining soil with running water.

Cleansing using other crystals

A large uncut piece of amethyst will cleanse and restore energies to any crystal you have used for healing, divination or to protect yourself from bad vibes. Wrap the crystal with the amethyst in dark silk, packing them both carefully so that they do not scratch each other You can also soak the amethyst and your healing crystal together in a glass container of rain water for 24 hours.

Cleansing using a herbal infusion

Hyssop, sage and peppermint are natural healers and protective herbs (see Psychic Protection in Nature, page 67). Hyssop is an especially good choice as a cleanser if a crystal has been given to you and you do not want any negative vibrations associated with the donor's life to be unwittingly transmitted along with the loving energies that prompted the gift. Sage improves clarity of thought and peppermint restores energy.

- Use one teaspoon of dried herb for 500 ml/17 fl oz/2¼ cups of water.
- If you are using fresh herbs, use 15 ml/1 tbsp of the leaves, chopped.
- Place the herbs in a pot, pour boiling water over and leave the infusion to cool.
- Strain the infusion into a ceramic or glass dish.
- Add the crystals you wish to cleanse and leave them for 12 hours.
- Hold them under running water to wash off any remaining infusion and allow to dry naturally.

Cleansing using an incense stick or cone
Pass the crystal nine times anti-clockwise over a cleansing incense to remove any negativity, and then nine times clockwise to restore its natural energies.

Incenses that are potent for purifying crystals include cypress, sweetgrass, frankincense, myrrh and pine.

Cleansing crystals with salt
Do not use this method with a crystal that is brittle or cracked.

- Sprinkle a few pinches of sea salt in a bowl of spring water.
- Make the sign of the cross, either the Christian form or the older astrological cross of the Mother Goddess (see page 19) in the water before adding the crystals.
- Leave the crystal in the salt solution for 12 hours and then rinse to remove all the salt before placing it to dry naturally. Seawater works as well.

Charging your crystals with positive power

Each of the methods I have described above will cleanse your crystals and also empower them at the same time. However, you may wish to add extra power if your crystals have to work hard.

You can empower several crystals at the same time. This is my own favourite method. You need to take the crystals to a sacred place of ancient power; this can be a standing stone, an old stone circle or one of the ancient healing wells formerly dedicated to the Mother Goddess that were

Christianised and rededicated to St Bride, the Virgin Mary or another Christian (often Celtic) saint. Go as early in the morning as possible.

- Wrap the crystals in white silk and place them on a flat surface, either on one of the stones or close to the water.

- Sit quietly, allowing the natural energies to fill your crystals (and yourself) with light and power; you may catch a misty image of one of the old grey or brown guardians of these places whose essence dates back to time immemorial. You may hear faint voices on the wind or find that the gentle rustling of leaves or the murmur of water from the well spring evokes images and words in your mind. Accept these – the oldest forms of divination came from interpreting natural sources and carried in-built protection, so you need have no fear.

- After about ten minutes, gently touch the crystals and you may feel a slight tingling: the work is done. If not, leave them a little longer and do nothing and say nothing, simply wait. (This is incredibly hard for a hyperactive person like me, but it is very important to allow positivity to take root, within you as well as your crystals.)

- Before you leave, thank the guardians of the place silently and you may be rewarded by a sudden breeze or a shimmering mistiness. I like to leave a flower or a crystal or a coin for someone else to find and take pleasure in, but some curators of sacred places do not welcome such offerings, so find out in advance. You can always leave your offering on a fence post or stone just outside the area – or choose a site that is entirely open. (In Sweden, where I have visited several of these sites, there is right of access and vandalism is non-existent.)

If you cannot visit an ancient site, there is an equally effective method you can use.

- Hold a crystal pendulum up to the bright sunlight (if there is no sun, hold it in front of a fibre optic lamp and swirl it so that it catches rainbows). Hold your pendulum in your power hand (the one you write with).

- With your other hand, hold the crystal you wish to charge beneath the pendulum so it catches the light and turn your pendulum nine times clockwise over the crystal to absorb power.

Another method is to take your crystal out at the time of the full moon (the two or three nights leading up to the full moon are also powerful). Hold your crystal up so that the light of the moon shines on it. Alternatively, fill a bowl with water and place it in the open air so that the moon is reflected in it. You can then bathe your crystal in empowering moonlight and leave to dry. You can also bathe a crystal in sunlight, but I find the Moon method more gently empowering for crystals that are primarily intended to act as guardians. But do experiment, as sun water may be best for you.

As these are personal crystals, you may ask the Moon or Sun to lend their power in your own words or you may prefer to remain silent and let these ancient forces work in their own way.

Using protective crystals

Protective crystals are perhaps the least obtrusive form of psychic security to incorporate into your everyday world. You can wear a crystal as a pendant or keep a cluster of crystals on your desk at work. If you have a room that always seems dark and inhospitable, place crystals in the four corners – their presence will not be noticeable, but their influence will be significant, none the less. You can also set crystals discreetly at the four corners of the table where you are carrying out divinatory or psychic work, to act as a psychic shield from negativity or debilitating emotions.

Crystals are particularly useful when you feel that you are vulnerable to attack, whether it be emotional, physical or psychic. Whenever you are faced with a particularly challenging situation, place all your crystals in a dish and hold your left hand over it for right-brain intuitive wisdom (the right side of the brain controls the left hand). With your eyes closed, allow your unconscious mind to select the crystal that you feel is most appropriate; this may not be the one that you would have selected consciously. However, your unconscious mind uses a psychic radar and afterwards you will realise you did select the best crystal for events that you might not have anticipated on a conscious level.

On a slightly more complicated level, you may also wish to carry out the following protective ritual, using seven crystals, after your psychic work or any time you feel vulnerable.

Seven, like nine, is traditionally held to be a very significant number. It occurs over and over again in the context of religious, magic and psychic ceremonies. It also represents the seven main chakras or psychic energy points associated with the human body (see Chakra and Aura Protection, page 153). This ritual is a good way of slowing down your energies when your mind is buzzing, especially at night or at any time you feel hostile energies projected towards you. It is a ritual I have used many times and found to be particularly effective, especially in hotel rooms after a long stressful journey. It has calmed my nerves on the night before an important broadcast and will also clear a room of bad vibes left by the previous occupant.

- You are going to make a circle of seven small crystals on the table or on the floor in front of you, placing the first one in magnetic north (use a compass to find it) at the 12 o'clock position of an imaginary clock face, and moving anti-clockwise. Sit in the south as you work. If you wish, you can form the crystal circle around yourself. Each crystal will be about 50 degrees apart.

- In the northernmost position, which traditionally represents the direction of midnight and winter, set a black crystal, such as an obsidian, or a soft black pebble. This denotes the boundary between the everyday world and other dimensions, and signifies your acceptance that there is a right time for every purpose. It will also shut out the unfair or depressing words of others that may still be invading your mind.

- Place a soft purple crystal, such as a sodalite or an amethyst, to the left of the first crystal, feeling all the magical energies from divination or the unfinished earthly projects passing into the cosmos and leaving your inner spirit at peace.

- Still working anti-clockwise, place a pale blue crystal, such as a blue lace agate or a moonstone, to banish all regrets and annoyance at all the words you have not spoken. Realise that some of the things that seem so important today may have paled into insignificance by tomorrow.

- Next, place a subtle green crystal, such as a jade or a moss agate, in the circle. This crystal fills your heart with love and sympathy even for those who have wronged you and prevents the quarrels and anxieties of others from intruding on your quiet time.

- A gentle yellow crystal, perhaps a yellow calcite or a rutilated quartz, is placed next in the circle. It encourages you to listen to your intuition and to leave to fade the demands of the outer world that cannot be resolved right now.

- A soft pink crystal, such as a rose quartz, placed next banishes unresolved anger or bitterness that may linger in your heart from the past.

- Finally, to the immediate right of the black crystal, a brown pebble brings you back to the mundane world; it carries with it total acceptance of what we all are, and so brings relaxation or rest.

Protective crystal wisdom

The following crystals absorb negative energies emanating from both personal fears and doubts and external attack, replacing them with positive emotions and intentions. Each has innate healing powers for specific aspects of body, mind and soul. As well as carrying, wearing and keeping your crystals close to you at work or home, you can also add a crystal to your bath water. Alternatively, soak it in pure spring water overnight and drink the crystalline water in the morning or carry it in a small bottle to splash on your face and wrists at stressful times. You can perhaps choose two or three crystals and make up the different waters to store on the fridge in a clear bottle. Clear crystal quartz water is both calming and energising. You can also dip your crystal in water and apply it to the centre of your brow (where your psychic third eye is located) to give you intuitive wisdom and clarity and to lift your own depression or inertia.

Agate
Colours: Opaque, red, orange, yellow, brown, black; may be banded or single-colour

Agates offer emotional and physical balance and bring stability to uncertain situations, promoting acceptance of self and others with faults and failings.

In Ancient Rome, agates were sacred to the gods of vegetation and even today the moss agate is associated with the restorative effects of nature, so connecting the user with the Earth and protecting during psychic work.

Agates are said to help screen out harmful X-rays and radiation.

Black agate protects against external negative forces.

Blue lace agate, which is pale blue and translucent, is the gentlest member of the agate family, calming strong emotions, creating a sense of peace and encouraging patience, especially with children and in situations that cannot be changed. Drinking water in which blue lace agate has been soaked for 12 hours ensures that kind, wise words are spoken. The crystal slows down hyperactivity in children and alleviates headaches if dipped in water and pressed on the brow.

Amber
Colours: Clear yellow, golden brown or orange

An organic gem, this is my own favourite protective stone, since it puts everything into perspective. Amber is petrified tree resin that can be up to 50 million years old and may contain the remains of plants, insects and even lizards. Because of its great antiquity and soft, warm touch, it is said to contain the power of many suns and so has the ability to absorb doubts and fears and also protect the user from external harm. It will also melt any emotional or physical rigidity within the self that can sometimes create inner conflict.

According to Chinese tradition, the souls of tigers pass into amber when they die and so it is also a gem of courage. Above all, it protects children, especially from falls (coral also does this). A powerful pathway to the past, it also improves short-term memory and can heal lingering sorrows.

It is believed to offer some protection from radiation, especially X-rays, the sun, computers and other industrial pollutants.

Amethyst

Colours: Pale lilac and lavender through to deep purple, translucent, semi-transparent and transparent

One of the most protective and healing stones. If you were to have only one protective stone, this would be the best choice, since it heals people, animals, plants and even other crystals.

Egyptian soldiers wore amethyst in battle so they would not lose their courage in dangerous situations, and in the same way amethysts will guide and comfort you through any dark night of the soul or actual crisis. The Greeks believed that amethysts prevented the wearer from drunkenness – and in the modern world an amethyst is still considered effective against alcohol, over-eating and other addictions.

Amethysts heal both mind and body, especially physical ailments caused by stress or long-term emotional pressures. At night, amethysts help to relieve insomnia and also prevent nightmares and night terrors in children; during the day, they minimise anger and impatience and so are a good crystal to put in your workplace or in a room before difficult visitors arrive. I have an amethyst pyramid I keep by the phone and I find this helps to calm me if a conversation becomes confrontational. Amethysts may also relieve headaches when placed on the temples or the point of pain.

Apache tear (Obsidian)

Colours: Black, semi-transparent

These small globules of obsidian are named after a Native American legend concerning a tragic incident in Arizona when a group of Apaches was ambushed. Many were killed and the rest threw themselves over a cliff, rather than be taken prisoner. The women and maidens of the tribe wept at the base of the cliff for a whole moon cycle and their tears became embedded within obsidian crystals.

Those who carry obsidian will never, it is said, know deep sorrow. When you hold your obsidian to the light, you can see new hope and life glimmering. Apache tears ease and release physical and mental pain, loss, sadness and anger; if they are worn regularly, cleansed and gently recharged in moonlight (a waxing moon is best for these crystals) they will gradually encourage the user to move forward and smile again. Obsidian absorbs dark energies and converts them to white healing light; hold your obsidian up to the light and see better days ahead.

Powerful for earthing, obsidian is an antidote to illusion and escapism. It absorbs and dissolves anger and protects sensitive people from unfair criticism. It also helps the user to release regrets for lost love or happiness; another stone for travellers.

Aquamarine
Colours: Clear light blue, blue-green to dark blue

The name means 'water of the sea' in Latin and has traditionally been the protective stone of sailors and fishermen. As a Water stone, it calms stress and comforts those who are grieving or in extreme mental or spiritual pain. It also fosters tolerance in situations that cannot be changed. If the crystal is placed in water overnight, and the water drunk first thing in the morning, the drink is said to cleanse the whole body.

Aquamarine encourages clear communication, creativity and confidence.

Beryl
Colours: Transparent, golden brown and pink

A crystal of the Sun, golden beryl improves and uplifts the spirit in difficult situations or where there are many factors to integrate. It alleviates stress-related conditions and counteracts exhaustion, depression, fear and resentment. Beryl is especially helpful in treating eating disorders, increasing self-esteem and self-love.

Pink beryl is a stone of gentle love and acceptance that provides stability and eases pressures in times of change. It is protective against nightmares and anxieties and is a good stone for children.

Bloodstone (Heliotrope)
Colours: Opaque, mottled green and red

In Ancient Babylon, bloodstone was used in amulets for protection against enemies. Bloodstone is primarily a stone of courage and was carried by soldiers in many cultures to overcome fears and to protect against wounding. The red spots were, according to legend, formed from the blood of Christ as it fell on green jasper at the crucifixion. Therefore this is a stone to carry if you fear enemies of any kind or face spite or malice. It also repels psychic attack.

Carnelian
Colours: Yellow, orange and red, occasionally brown, also translucent

Carnelian is also a stone of courage and self-confidence and is very protective as well as empowering, repelling envy and malice. In the Middle

Ages, carnelian amulets were engraved with symbols of classical heroes and heroines to give a home protection against storms, lightning and fire.

Carnelian also helps with food-related problems, phobias and other compulsive behaviour, especially where a question of identity and self-esteem is involved.

Coral
Colours: Opaque, red and orange

An organic gem, coral has been considered a protective stone for children from the time of the Ancient Greeks. Plato wrote that coral should be hung around children's necks to prevent them falling and to cure colic, and rubbed on the gums to help painless teething.

Coral is also potent in guarding adults; it will turn paler if the wearer is ill or exhausted and return to its normal colour when health is restored. Coral was also nailed to ships' masts to protect them from storms. It encourages fertility, and energises body and mind.

Pink coral offers emotional support in times of uncertainty.

White coral alleviates stress.

Black coral protects against self-destructive instincts.

Desert rose
Colours: Light brown, rough-textured, opaque with glints

This not an immediately attractive stone: it resembles a walnut rather than a crystal. However, desert rose is the stone of all who wander far from home or seek inner understanding. It contains an inner store of wisdom; it is an earthing stone that reduces anxiety and calms racing thoughts.

Diamond
Colours: Transparent sparkling white jewel, also yellow, brown, orange, pink, lavender, blue, green and occasionally black

During the Middle Ages, diamonds were worn to prevent plague. African medicine men and women have long carried these stones in their healing bundles and that is how outsiders first became aware of their existence.

A diamond removes physical and emotional blockages and negativity and is said to draw toxicity from the body. It also preserves fidelity between lovers.

It is a good energiser when exhaustion or doubts set in.

Emerald
Colours: Green, sparkling, transparent, though can sometimes be cloudy

The Romans believed that emeralds were a warning stone and lost their colour or even crumbled when evil was near and so they acquired a reputation for protection, especially against treachery and infidelity.

As stones of Venus, emeralds are also endowed with powerful healing properties, for relieving emotional troubles, depression, stress-related conditions and insomnia.

Fluorite
Colours: Rainbow shades

Fluorite in all shades is protective, bringing harmony to mind and body and traditionally helping to heal physical and emotional scars, as well as being effective for detoxification, anxiety, and insomnia.

Blue fluorite encourages us to forgive our own mistakes and omissions.

Clear and purple fluorite cleanse the auric field and clear away stagnant energies, preparing the way for new experiences.

Green fluorite stills an over-active mind, and is especially good for transition points in life.

Garnet
Colours: Clear, red to dark red, also green, orange and colourless

Primarily a protective stone. Eastern European peoples traditionally used the garnet against illness, night phantoms and all forms of evil, including the mythical vampire. In medieval times, garnets were engraved with a lion's head for health and safe travel, and the garnet is still regarded as a stone for travellers, especially against attack. Like the emerald, it will change colour if danger is near.

Garnets also provide energy when rest is not possible.

Haematite
Colours: Silver-grey, metallic brilliance

A powerful earthing and protective stone that activates natural survival instincts. The Ancient Egyptians used it to soothe hysteria and worries. Strongly linked to the physical body, haematitite acts as a shield against potential physical and emotional hostility.

Jade
Colours: Many shades of green, opaque to translucent

Jade is a stone that protects children because of its gentleness and, like the amethyst, it heals people, animals and plants, being especially associated with vegetation and the growing energies of the garden.

A stone for health, prosperity and long life, jade was associated with reincarnation in the Orient; it calms emotions and encourages kindness, especially in the family and with children.

Jasper
Colours: Opaque, multi-coloured, single colours, yellow, orange, brown, green, also sometimes found as petrified wood

A powerful earthing and protective stone in all its colours and central to all forms of psychic self-defence.

Black jasper is protective against all negativity, especially the user's own repressed feelings. It is good for absorbing anger coming from others, so that you do not turn it against yourself.

Brown jasper offers stability in turbulent times; it is good to use after rituals and divination to bring you back to earth; brown jasper increases the acuity of the five earthly senses and so is good if you fear deception by others.

Green jasper protects against jealousy, increases empathy with others' difficulties, soothes bad dreams.

Leopardskin jasper is really good for shedding what is redundant in your life; it can bring what you need, rather than what you think would make you happy.

Red jasper offers a defence against all hostility.

Yellow jasper is good for grounding and for acceptance of others and life as they really are; it prevents resentment building up.

Jet
Colour: Black

An organic gem, jet is fossilised wood that has been turned into a dense form of coal, and so, like amber, is of great antiquity. It is a very protective stone against sorrow and all forms of negativity and has been used from early times as an amulet.

Powdered jet was for many centuries taken in water to cure toothache, and as an ointment for skin troubles and to give protection against the bites of snakes and scorpions.

A stone that will guard travellers and fishermen from all harm, jet amulets were kept at home by the wives of sailors so that their husbands would return safely from the sea. Jet prevents nightmares and is said to help the user to face the natural ending of a phase, and move on to the next.

Kunzite
Colours: Pink, lilac, transparent

A potent stone, sometimes known as the 'woman's stone', because of its ability to soothe all female disorders and sorrows, kunzite also allows the expression of *anima* (female) qualities in men. Kunzite increases compassion and the ability to give unconditional love to oneself as well as others. Good for overcoming compulsive behaviour and addictions, it restores confidence and reduces depression. For our modern world, this is the crystal to keep in the car, for protecting against road rage and tensions, and at work to keep stress at bay.

Lapis lazuli
Colours: Opaque rich medium to dark blue with flecks of iron pyrites (fool's gold)

Known as the 'eye of wisdom', the stone of the gods, lapis lazuli is mentioned in an Ancient Egyptian papyrus from over 3,000 years ago as having healing and protective powers. The Sumerians believed it contained the souls of their gods and goddesses and as such would endow them with magical powers and the protection of the deities themselves.

In Egypt, lapis lazuli was used first in a powdered form for eye make-up and women would then circle their eyes with the powder as protection against the evil eye. So this is a stone that has retained its reputation for protection against malevolence from spirit as well as earthly sources.

Malachite
Colour: Opaque green with black stripes

A purifier and energiser that replaces negativity, anger and depression with positive energies, and physical and emotional pain with warmth and a sense of well-being. Malachite cleanses the auric field, and is also noted for absorbing pollution and the harmful, enervating energies from computers, faxes, mobile phones and televisions; malachite crystals can, for the same reason, be placed in the corners of a room where domestic electrical goods are in constant use. Because it works so hard, malachite should be cleansed at least every two days.

Moonstone or selenite
Colours: Translucent white, fawn, pink, yellow, occasionally blue

Moonstone is believed to absorb the powers of the Moon, becoming deeper in colour, more translucent and more powerful for healing and protection as the moon waxes until it reaches full moon.

Moonstone is a protector of travellers, especially by night or at sea, and is potent against night terrors, nightmares and all supernatural malevolence; it is especially good for soothing hormonal mood swings.

Mother of pearl
Colour: Silvery white and shimmering with rainbow colours

An organic gem, made of the glossy, pearlised interior of pearl oyster shells, mother of pearl is very protective for young children and babies, particularly during their first months of life. It carries the peaceful healing energy of the sea, soothes extremes of emotions and prevents the user from absorbing negativity. It is especially good for healing difficult relationships between mothers and children of any age.

Obsidian *see Apache tear*

Snowflake obsidian
Colour: Black with white spots

Assists acceptance of our shadow side and basic instincts as part of whole self and enables us to channel personal negativity into positive change and action.

Quartz, crystal
Colours: Transparent or semi-transparent, in a variety of colours, less commonly cloudy or opaque

If there could be only one healing and energising stone, it would be clear crystal quartz. This crystal has been recognised in all times and cultures as a powerful transmitter of physical and psychic energies, and regarded by peoples as far apart as the Australian Aborigines, the Chinese and the Native Americans as manifestation of the living creative spirit. It is easily charged and cleansed, and will amplify the energies of the user, drawing out negative energies and creating positive ones in their place. Clear crystal quartz triggers the body's own immune system to resist infection and negativity.

Rose quartz, a translucent to clear pink crystal, is the stone of gentle healing and protection, especially for babies, children, very old people, the sick and all who are vulnerable; rose quartz soothes away sorrows and banishes nightmares and night terrors in children and adults alike. It promotes family love and friendship, brings peace, forgiveness and the mending of quarrels, healing emotional wounds and heartbreak, grief, stress, fear, lack of confidence, resentment and anger; it is especially good for dissolving sorrows left from childhood. Rose quartz works better set in silver than gold.

Cleanse and recharge your rose quartz frequently, especially if the colour begins to fade.

Rutilated or rutile quartz has metallic, golden rutile, copper, or blue/grey titanium fibres through it. According to legend, it was created when angels froze the water of the heavens and it is said that guardian angels dwell in the crystals, offering protection and wise counsel to users. Rutilated quartz alleviates all inner ills, emotional and physical, and amplifies healing energy and thoughts. The golden kind, in particular, boosts natural immunity and can help to break emotionally draining behaviour patterns, especially unresolved issues left from childhood.

Smoky quartz has grey or brown transparent crystals. It is traditionally associated with weakening negative influences on the user, and assists in acknowledging and dealing with personal anger and resentment rather than denying negative feelings or projecting them on to others; it alleviates anxiety, depression and destructive emotional patterns, and fosters creativity and joy.

Ruby
Colour: Sparkling red

Legend has it that rubies contain living flames and can be used to boil water. The stone of kings and emperors, and sacred to Buddha and Krishna, the ruby links mind, body and spirit and offers access to the collective wisdom of mankind.

Ruby is another warning gem, changing colour when illness or anger threatens the owner. However, a ruby intensifies all emotions, especially love and passion but also jealousy and impatience, and so should be used with care. It offers protection against storms at home if placed in each of the corners of the house.

Sapphire
Colours: Sparkling blue, green, pink, purple and clear

Related to the ruby, sapphires are potent against envy. The Greeks believed that the sapphire was sacred to Apollo, and so the gem has come to symbolise wisdom and also joy. It is a stone of fidelity, between friends or lovers, and of chastity and purity of thought. It is therefore a good stone for all matters of love, or where trust is an issue. Sapphires also bring mental clarity, clearing confusion and redundant guilt and resentments.

Blue sapphires increase communication with spirit guides or guardian angels; they act as a repository of conscious and unconscious wisdom, will-power, optimism and inspiration, and as an anti-depressant.

Star sapphires are more subtle in their effects, reducing anxiety levels and indecision, and shielding against pollutants of all kinds.

Sodalite
Colours: Deep blue, purple, often with white flecks, white and indigo

Alleviates subconscious guilt and fears; offers protection from negative energies of all kinds; placed next to computers, faxes, etc., sodalite is believed to reduce the effects of harmful rays from technological and electrical equipment.

Sugilite
Colour: Opaque, rich purple

Absorbs negativity from the wearer's aura and replaces it with positive energies. A relatively expensive stone but valuable for healing, sugilite relieves headaches, reduces stress levels and removes toxins and emotional blocks. Placed on the brow at the level of the third eye, the crystal will alleviate depression and feelings of worthlessness or despair; a bringer of peace and spiritual enlightenment.

Tiger's eye
Colours: Yellow-gold and brown stripes, burgundy-striped, chatoyant (reflecting light in a wavy band)

Tiger's eye combines the powers of the Earth with the deep instinctive ability to survive life's challenges. Throughout the ages, tiger's eye has been a talisman against the evil eye. Roman soldiers would wear these engraved stones as protection from death and wounding. Tiger's eye is, above all, a stone of balance in the body, damping desire for excesses of food, alcohol or nicotine; emotionally, it offers a sense of perspective and the ability to see other people's point of view.

Topaz
Colours: Clear, sparkling, golden, champagne-coloured, pink, pale blue, orange or brown

The name means 'fire' in Sanskrit. Topaz increases power with the waxing of the moon, being at its greatest potency at the time of the full moon. Perhaps because of this, topaz was said to be proof against supernatural creatures of the night, nightmares and night terrors.

Water in which a topaz has been soaked is a cure for insomnia if drunk an hour before bedtime. It is also good for lowering one's profile in potentially hazardous or confrontational situation (the ancients of the East believed it actually conferred invisibility on the wearer). It is especially good for defusing violent emotions whether in oneself or others.

Golden topaz helps in letting go of the past, controls anxiety conditions and lessens mood swings, physical exhaustion and emotional distress; it is especially good for alleviating work anxieties and so should be kept in the workplace.

Tourmaline
Colours: Black, blue, green, pink, watermelon (green, pink and red striped), striated, clear or semi-transparent

Endows protective light on the wearer. Dispels fear, negativity and sorrows and encourages peaceful sleep.

Black tourmaline protects the wearer against hostile feelings and negative intentions of others; it can be used after psychic or healing work to restore the connection with the everyday world, without losing connection with psychic insights gained; it is also good for diminishing the power of neuroses and obsessions.

Blue tourmaline increases patience in difficult situations or with trouble-some people; establishes links with one's Higher Self and angelic and spirit guides through divination, meditation or psychic work for wise guidance.

Green tourmaline balances personal emotions so that they do not drain physical energies. It energises, restoring enthusiasm and optimism, and brings increase to all spheres, not least compassion.

Pink tourmaline endows love of self and others, heals emotional as well as physical pain, gives comfort and relief in chronic illness and removes old sorrows and redundant regrets; balances natural desire for peace with necessary assertiveness for well-being.

Turquoise
Colours: Opaque, light blue/blue-green

Mined by the Egyptians in Sinai more than 6,000 years ago, turquoise is a stone of power. If placed in a saddle or on a bridle, it may be used by riders to warn them of danger and to prevent horses stumbling. Famed also as a protection against poison, turquoise is reputed to change colour if poison or other dangers are near.

Turquoise also absorbs all negative forces and helps to detoxify the system of alcohol, pollution, X-rays and radiation from the sun; it is said to be effective in alleviating anorexia and food-related disorders, migraines and anxiety. Turquoise is said to work better if set in silver rather than gold.

Crystal protection for your animal

There are many hazards facing household pets, especially those that go out of doors, including predators, infections, hostile neighbours and traffic. Animals can be stolen or lured away and even microchips do not offer complete protection as some people consider them a limitation on the freedom of an animal, preferring to be able to disappear if it does not wish to stay. A traditional protective device is to tie a tiny turquoise crystal to the animal's collar.

Equally effective as turquoise is a shiny bell, like the horse brass of old, to repel negativity and return it to the sender. Animals do have quite a strong sense of danger but as they become domesticated and increasingly humanised by their owners, this becomes less acute. Therefore it is quite important for any protective amulet to make connection with the earth to reactivate the wild animal's natural ability to, for example, eat a herb it knows instinctively will cure an illness.

- Place the crystal or bell in soil in which moss agate or jade, the gardener's crystals, have been placed and in which is growing a gently protective and healing plant such as chamomile, eau de cologne, or lavender. Leave it there for 24 hours, if possible the day before the full moon or any waxing moon day, from dawn to the following dawn.

- Wash the crystal or bell under running water, if possible from a natural outdoor source.

- Leave it high in the air, out of doors, for a further 24 hours beginning at dawn this time, preferably on the day of the full moon early in the moon cycle.

- Finally, at noon the following day, you can dedicate it with fire. Once more, if possible, work out of doors, using a small fire in a large, metal container, a pit or a barbecue. Pass the amulet over the flame once and then circle the flame with it four more times, saying:

Fire of one, keep – (name pet) safe from all sickness, injury and infection.
Fire of two, drive away all thieves and predators, human and animal.
Fire of three, keep distant vehicles, machinery
and all perils of the modern world.
Fire of four, keep – from straying unless he/she wishes to do so
and may this fire light the way home.
Fire of five, let those with hate in their heart not come near
and let – not stray where he is not welcomed with love.

- Finally, with your amulet in the right hand, scatter four handfuls of dried rosemary or bay on to the fire, saying:

> *Fires of six, seven, eight and nine,*
> *Bring joy and long life to this friend of mine.*

- Suspend the crystal or bell from the collar or in the case of birds from a mirror in a cage or aviary.

- As the animal moves, the bell will jingle, dispelling any hostile energies.

- If you are using the ritual for a horse, bind the amulet with three hairs from the horse's mane before beginning.

Protective metals

All metals are protective, since they are extracted from the Earth and so carry its power within them. Even metal alloys carry the potency of their source metal.

Since Ancient Babylonian times, particular metals have been associated with the five ancient planets known to the early astronomers, and with the Sun and the Moon and their ruling deities. In Western alchemy, it was believed that when the influence of the ruling planet was strong, its metal would grow much faster within the Earth. The metals, sometimes called by their planetary names, were said to contain an *arcanum*, a celestial power derived directly from the ruling planet. This arcanum, having been released and perfected through alchemical processes, was thought to provide a highly effective medicine.

It is these magical associations that have caused metals to become so closely linked with amulets and talismans, a power that in the case of iron and brass has extended to ordinary household objects made of them. Power and protection are very closely entwined in magical metal lore, and so each metal offers an antidote to the negative qualities of its associated planet.

You may find it helpful to collect coins or small objects of each of the planetary metals or their substitute to carry as protective amulets or use as a focus in protective rituals.

In earlier times, coins were considered healing and protective because on them was depicted originally the head of a deity or, from medieval times, a monarch to whom healing powers were attributed. Coins with holes, for example Chinese divinatory coins or the soon to be obsolete Spanish 25 peseta coin, are especially protective and luck-attracting. Pendants, too, in different metals endow the wearer with the planetary qualities, especially if engraved with the planetary glyph (see pages 106–9).

You can also entwine your zodiacal glyph with its ruling or co-ruling planet (see pages 43–6) in the appropriate metal.

Metals and their planetary qualities

Sun

The Sun rules **Leo**. Its metals are **gold** and **brass**.

Gold contains the pure *animus* (male) power and energy for success and achievement. It protects against poverty, failure, bad luck, envy, ill-health, pettiness and spite, inner fears and depression. In India, children wear small golden charms to keep them from all harm, and sailors in many countries used to wear a single gold earring for the same reason.

Gold is a particularly special talisman for men, for young people setting out in life and for all who aim high.

Brass offers a cheaper alternative to gold and is also a very protective metal. It is used to reflect back negativity to the sender. Horse brasses were placed on horses' bridles to keep away any harmful spirits and to deflect the evil eye. Metallic protective symbols worn by horses date back more than 5,000 years. Horse brasses would be handed down by carters, from father to son. They are often in the shape of moons, suns or stars, to invoke the brightness of the celestial spheres, and both the shiny surface and the jingling sound of these and brass bells on the harness were a powerful deterrent for harm.

The shiny surface of brass, especially hanging in hallways of homes and on brass door knockers and steps, was the way our forebears reflected back any hostile influences that sought to enter the home; brass bells protected European homes long before the protective wind chimes that are so common today infiltrated from the East.

☽ Moon

The Moon rules **Cancer**. Its metal is **silver**.

Silver contains the pure *anima* (female) power of intuition, of instinctive wisdom, spiritual and psychic understanding. From time immemorial, silver has been used for images of goddesses, and silver bells are a special invocation of the power of all Mother Goddesses.

Silver offers protection against psychic attack (werewolves could, it was said, be killed with a silver bullet), against bad dreams and night terrors, compulsions and addictions, and against illusion and secret enemies. It also guards those who travel at night or by sea. It is especially protective for women, babies and young children.

☿ Mercury

Mercury rules **Gemini** and **Virgo**. Its metals are **mercury** and **aluminium**.

Mercury contains the ability to communicate and learn new things, to interact with others and to adapt to the needs of the moment. Mercury protects against trickery, misleading communications, fickleness, mental cruelty, unfair criticism, sarcasm, computer hacking and business failure. It is especially protective towards travellers on short journeys.

Aluminium may be substituted for mercury, as mercury is highly toxic.

♀ Venus
Venus rules **Taurus** and **Libra**. Its metal is **copper**.

Copper possesses the power to attract love and to encourage harmonious relationships with family and friends as well as lovers. The natural healing powers of copper are attributed to its ability to balance the body's polarity. Copper bracelets are still worn to prevent and relieve rheumatism and arthritis, a custom that began in the Middle Ages.

Copper protects against illness, family quarrels, jealousy, pollution and environmental destruction, infidelity, cruel lovers and emotional blackmail. Copper protects lovers, children and animals.

♂ Mars
Mars rules **Aries** and is the co-ruler of **Scorpio**. Its metals are **iron** and **steel**.

Iron offers the courage to stand against injustice and traditionally provides protection against negative influences, both earthly and paranormal.

Iron gained its magical associations as metal of the gods, and especially the gods of war, when it was first discovered in meteors that fell to the ground in balls of fire and so was seen as a gift from the deities. Iron nails were driven into the beds of women in labour and into infants' cradles as protection against spirits who might do harm; a child's first bath water would be run over the blade of an iron scythe before being poured over him or her, to stave off illness and enchantment, since fairies and bad witches were believed to fear iron.

A piece of iron or an iron or steel object, such as a pair of scissors, would be buried under the threshold of a new home to prevent negative influences entering the home. Alternatively, iron would be buried near the front door with just the tip showing, so that it would deflect any unfriendly vibrations. These would pass into the Earth and be absorbed to be regenerated as positive growth (see page 28 for an iron ritual).

Iron defends the user against physical violence and cruelty, anger and viciousness. It is the guardian of all who fight for good causes, mentally or physically of adolescents and of those approaching transitions in their life.

Steel has similar properties to iron and, like brass, is good for reflecting back negativity.

♃ Jupiter

Jupiter rules **Sagittarius** and is co-ruler of **Pisces**. Its metal is **tin**.

Tin provides wisdom, optimism and the expansion of horizons. Tin ingots and artefacts have been excavated in lake dwellings that are thousands of years old and, because it is so malleable, tin has been used to engrave talismans for good fortune from early times. The metal has been used for divination, with molten tin being cast in water to make shapes from which the future could be foretold. It is also used in money rituals because many ancient coins were made of tin.

Tin protects against injustice, corrupt or intractable officialdom, autocrats and bullies, unfairness at work and natural disasters. Jupiter, especially, protects mature people, those in committed emotional relationships or work partnerships and the vulnerable at any age or stage.

Occasionally bronze, metal of the Mother Goddess, is substituted for tin.

♄ Saturn

Saturn rules **Capricorn** and is co-ruler of **Aquarius**. Its metal is **lead** or **pewter**.

Lead offers mastery over fate, through recognising the need to work within an actual, and not ideal, situation with the resources tools available and finding a way round difficulties.

Lead was traditionally placed above the threshold of a house to prevent harmful influences entering the home. Lead was also the metal used for written offerings and charms in the classical world, for power, protection and fertility.

Curses were written on tablets of lead and cast into water. Examples of this could be seen at the Roman baths in Avon, England, that were sacred to the Romano-Celtic goddess Sulis Minerva.

Lead protects against the pollution caused by X-rays, electricity and noise; it also guards against sorrow, grief, destructive relationships of all kinds and against hostility at home and seemingly random disasters. It is the guardian of those who are older, all who are grieving and any who are imprisoned by circumstances or reversals in fortune.

Pewter is the modern substitute for lead, which has to be handled with care, especially by children, as it is poisonous and relatively soluble.

Metals and the days of the week

According to tradition, each metal is sacred to a particular day of the week through its association with the planetary deities. On its special day, a metal's symbolic powers are especially potent.

You can carry a small coin, charm or amulet made of the relevant protective metal with you in a small drawstring bag on the metal's own day, or on a different day of the week, if you need the strength of that particular metal. For example, if you needed the courage of iron (whose day is Tuesday) on a Friday (which is the day of copper), you would carry your iron amulet, plus the copper. This would have the bonus of making you assertive, yet not hurting feelings, since Friday is the day of Venus.

The metals and their days of the week are as follows:

Sunday: Gold or brass

Monday: Silver

Tuesday: Iron

Wednesday: Mercury or aluminium

Thursday: Tin (occasionally bronze)

Friday: Copper

Saturday: Lead or pewter

Metal rings

Metal rings have long been worn for healing and protective purposes. For example, in the time of Edward the Confessor and throughout the Middle Ages, cramp rings, made of iron or bronze and blessed by the monarch, were believed to cure various diseases of the joints, especially cramp and rheumatism, and to offer protection against infections. They were sometimes fashioned from coins presented on Good Friday, in a similar ceremony to the Maundy Thursday money ceremony which takes place every year in the UK, when the monarch still presents coins to chosen people. Cramp rings were also said to be powerful if made from the hinges, handle or nails of a coffin, because their close association with death gave the wearer protection from potentially fatal illnesses. On a more romantic note, a suitor would place a pair of cramp rings in a swallow's nest for nine days and then deliver one of the pair to his intended, wearing the other until she came to him.

Rings of copper, a metal that is sacred to Hindus, are worn to offer protection against the demon that causes sciatica.

Protective rings

Circles are the most basic form of sacred geometry and have been used throughout history, symbolising life without end and perfection. So rings and also bracelets are a good way of absorbing the power of the different metals. As I said earlier in the book, the first jewellery was probably crafted as protective amulets.

You may choose or be given a ring containing a protective stone and wear it on the traditional heart, or wedding, finger, which is symbolically linked with the heart. Such a ring will always be special and accumulate great power as you wear it; this is the reason why many older people are reluctant ever to remove a wedding ring even for a moment, in case it breaks the union.

However, for the purposes of protective magic, you will need seven rings or discs with holes in them, one for each of the seven metals or their substitutes. You can find an array of such rings in museum gift shops and in mineral or craft outlet stores; alternatively, you could explore your local DIY store, or even look on the Internet. Museum shops are an excellent source of rings that copy the styles of many different periods, as well as coins, and they are usually remarkably cheap. Note that for this purpose a bronze ring is more durable than tin for Jupiter energies, and that pewter is the safe choice for Saturn. Stainless steel rings are a good substitute for iron and easier to wear.

You can wear, or carry in a charm bag, the ring of the most appropriate metal for your need or the metal associated with a particular day of the week.

Charging your protective rings

Rings are traditionally charged at dawn by using salt, oil, fire, flowers and gems or crystals.

- You can charge all your rings at the same time. Place them in a small glass or crystal dish.

- Sprinkle over them just two or three drops of an oil of the Sun (sunflower oil, pure cold-pressed olive oil, apricot and St John's Wort oil will all do), saying:

  I charge you with the power of the Sun to transform darkness into light, exhaustion into energy and despair into creativity, endowing me with the gold of inner as well as outer wealth.
  Turn away all negative, destructive powers that deplete joy, confidence and hope.

- Surround the dish with a circle of six (the number of Venus) green candles, saying as you light them:

  I charge you with the power of Venus to endow these rings with the power of love, friendship, affection, fidelity and trust.
  Turn away all hostile, cold and wounding words, all spite, envy and stifling possessiveness.

- Between the first and second candles, place a small rose quartz crystal for love.

- Between the second and third candles, place a tiger's eye for prosperity.

- Between the third and fourth candles, place an orange carnelian for fertility.

- Between the fourth and the fifth candles, place a green jade for health.

- Between the fifth and sixth candles, place a black obsidian for protection.

- Between the sixth and first candles, place a clear crystal quartz for pure light and the integration of the other energies.

(If you do not have any of these crystals, substitute any others or glass nuggets of the same colour.)

- When the candles are alight and the crystals in place, add a pinch of salt to the dish for health, protection and prosperity, saying:

  I charge you with the properties of the salt of the Earth, that give and preserve life and health, to bring protection, healing and sufficiency to my home and those I love.
  Turn away all sickness and destructive habits and obsessions.

- Finally, take a flower of the Moon, for example, jasmine, mimosa or any white flower or one that blossoms after dark. Petal by petal, add it to the dish of rings saying:

  I charge you with the power of the Moon, with the new beginnings and restorative energies of the new moon, the fertility of the full moon and the abandonment of old redundant sorrows and angers on the waning lunar disc.
  Turn away all external terrors of the night and the fears within that may haunt and paralyse me into inaction.

- Let the candles burn and leave the rings in the dish for 24 hours.

- On the new dawn, wash the rings in running water and wear the one associated with the particular day. If you use tin rather than bronze for your Jupiter ring, you may need to be careful when you wash it – it is best just to sprinkle it with two or three drops of water.

PSYCHIC PROTECTION LIFTS THE SPIRIT

- Wrap the rest of the rings in white silk and keep them in a small wooden box or bag made from natural fibres, with a sprig of lavender or dried rose petals.

- If possible, spend the day in calm, happy activities.

If you do have a bad day, you can cleanse your ring of any bad vibes: sprinkle it with salt, then hold it in the smoke of a cleansing incense such as rosemary, pine, or juniper. Pass it though a the flame of a golden candle and finally hold it for a few seconds under running water, saying such words as:

Let all that is not golden, let all that is not beautiful, let all that is not harmonious, let all that is not healing, leave this ring.
May there remain only love and light and healing.

In time, you will find that wearing or carrying your rings will attract positive energies – some would call this good luck – towards you, because you are open to good vibrations; negative feelings or bad luck will be repelled. You can also use this ritual to charge lucky coins and other metal amulets.

You can use your small metal objects, coins or pendants in the same way.

A *ritual with seven metals for driving away all darkness*

There are times when we feel threatened or overwhelmed by impossible odds and perhaps conventional sources of support are unavailable or simply do not seem to be helping.

This ritual is best carried out on any day when the moon is waxing, as close to noon as you can to benefit from solar and lunar energies. Alternatively, you can work on a clear night as the stars appear and identify those of the planets that are visible from a star map. You will need seven objects – one made of each of the planetary metals: gold for the Sun, silver for the Moon, mercury or aluminium for Mercury, copper for Venus, iron for Mars, tin for Jupiter and pewter for Saturn, or Old Father Time, as he was known.

- Go to an open space where you will be private and if possible find an especially protective tree, such as rowan, hazel or ash.

- On a stone, scratch a symbol or word that represents your fear or sorrow or, if the source of your angst is unknown, a question mark.

- Bury the stone at the foot of the tree, facing the west, the Celtic direction of endings and death – in this case, the death of your fears.

- If you cannot work out of doors, take a tree branch inside your home. Hawthorn is the only tree that should not be taken indoors, except on May Day. You can bury your stone in a pot, filled with soil and planted with a protective herb such as lavender.

- Take a dish of mixed parsley, sage, rosemary and thyme, traditional magical herbs of protection and empowerment.

- Beginning in the north, circle the tree clockwise, scattering herbs and saying:

Parsley, sage, rosemary, thyme,
By power of gold, make protection mine.

- Now pick up the gold object or disc and tie it to the tree with red cord. If it is too big, place it at the foot of the tree.

- Scatter a second circle of herbs, saying:

Parsley, sage, rosemary, thyme
By power of silver, make protection mine.

- Tie the silver object to a branch of the tree or at place it at its foot.

- Scatter a third circle of herbs and say:

Parsley, sage, rosemary, thyme,
By power of aluminium, make protection mine.

- The ritual continues until seven circles of herbs have been scattered round the tree, the seven metals named and all seven metals are on or around the base of the tree.

- Make a final chant with your arms outstretched, facing the south – the direction of full power – if it is daytime, or east for the coming dawn if you are working at night, saying:

Sun, Moon, Mercury, Venus, Mars, Jupiter and old Father Time,
By your sacred powers. protection is mine.

If possible leave the objects on the tree for 24 hours but, if not, collect them in a basket and leave them in the moonlight until the moon begins to wane.

SEVEN

Protection Against Psychic Attack

There are many different types of psychic attack, but in general they can be divided into two camps: the type that come from within us and those that come from external forces. Of course, there is a fine line between them and it can be hard to distinguish the true source of any psychic attack. It may be easy to identify those fears that arise from our brain as we consciously try to resolve current problems; but what about when we find ourselves prey to old fears and hurts we thought were long resolved? Have these been resurrected by our unconscious brain, as it re-enacts these buried episodes from our past at times of stress; or is it that an external malevolence from a known or unknown source is being directed at us?

Both may be experienced as a panic attack during the day: perhaps you misplace one thing after another in a short space of time, drop and break articles, cut or bump yourself; at night you may fall prey to violent nightmares from which you cannot wake and in which your body may feel paralysed. Sometimes the two sources of negativity are linked: we become less resistant to external spite or malice if we are tired or worried, and if we are on the receiving end of vicious words or thoughts, our inner fears and free-floating anxieties will be magnified. If we accept that there are malevolent forces, within and maybe beyond humanity, then psychic attack is quite possible. However, by far the majority of bad energies emanate from earthly sources and are caused by resentment, envy or jealousy.

Some apparently psychic attacks, especially those that manifest themselves in nightmares, may be a reflection of our own doubts or unhappiness projected in our minds as an external monster or demon. If you have a particular fear or phobia, suddenly the focus of your fear seems to appear in the most unlikely situations and places, almost as if your fears are drawing it towards you, like a magnet. But I have also noticed that if someone is feeling or acting spitefully towards me, then those hostile energies can draw me towards to the things I fear the most – and that only increases the phobia which makes it ever easier for my enemies to see me as a victim.

But all this can be short-circuited by repelling attack at an early stage, leaving you calm and your enemies reeling, as their malice comes hurtling back at them, threefold, at the speed of light.

Whether a threat is external and/or deliberately caused, or it is unconscious resentment that is winging your way, it is important, first of all, to limit your own (understandably) negative response. If you can avoid adding to the bad vibes, then you can prevent your auric field becoming tangled up in the bad feelings. Think of the negativity as a tennis ball that you can hit straight back, rather than an egg that splatters everywhere and takes ages to clean up. It is all too easy for an ordinary quarrel or bad feeling over some small act of injustice to become magnified until the plates start flying off the draining board apparently of their own volition.

Therefore, it is best to carry out a simple ritual to contain and minimise your own reactions. Once you have resolved your own negative feelings, it is much easier to put your psychic defence mechanisms in place.

A *ritual to resolve negativity*

This is a useful ritual for melting your own negative feelings, such as anger, jealousy or resentment, away.

- Take ice from a freezer, or ice cubes, and place them in a glass or metal bowl in a warm room.

- Take six pink candles, the colour and number of Venus in her gentler aspect, for love and reconciliation, and light them one by one, saying the following:

I light the first candle for peace.
Let there be peace in my heart
And peace to those who feel hostility towards me.

I light the second candle for generosity.
Let gifts willingly flow to those who need them
And compassion to those who steal what is not theirs.

I light the third candle for tolerance.
Let me tolerate those who think and act differently
And endow tolerance on those who feel offended by my beliefs.

I light the fourth candle for kindness.
Let me speak only gentle words and perform loving deeds
And send kindness to those who are harsh towards me.

I light the fifth candle for understanding.
Let me understand the hearts and intentions of others
And grant understanding to those who misrepresent me.

I light the sixth candle for love.
Help me to feel love to those who have hurt me
And fill my enemies' hearts with compassion.

- Let the ice melt in its own time. Sit in the candlelight and write, telephone or e-mail, first people who make you feel positive about yourself and then, as the ice thaws, those who are lonely and would welcome contact, even if this is difficult. Write only positive thoughts and send only good news.

- When the ice has melted, stir it nine times anti-clockwise with a wooden spoon, as you do so naming any sorrows or fears.

- Then tip the water into the earth where plants are growing, saying:

Sorrow, anger, flow from me, flow, not into the sea,
But to the earth to bring new birth, hope and positivity.

This principle is true of all psychic work, and if you only ever carry out rituals or divination when you are feeling positive, then you will be quite safe psychically and emotionally. The small proportion of attacks from other-worldly sources, during and after psychic work, are usually the result of people dabbling casually with the forces, perhaps playing with a ouija board or summoning up spirits in a séance. The kind of spirit who will appear through a glorified party game is going to be a less benign essence that may cause mischief or give frightening messages. Even if the nasty messages are coming from within your own mind, or from another person at the séance playing tricks, then the psychological effects can be quite devastating.

Later in this book I shall examine a range of methods for keeping harmful or emotionally draining energies away from you and your loved ones during your everyday life. In contrast, in this chapter I concentrate on the deliberate, malicious aspect of the phenomenon and suggest means of repelling actual psychic attacks from those who wish you ill.

I myself have been under psychic attack, once from a woman who was having an affair with my ex-husband and, more recently, from a woman who was jealous of what she saw as my success as a writer. In both cases, the people concerned made themselves known to me – it is unusual for a psychic attack to come from a totally unknown source and generally the attacker is unable to resist the temptation to find out if you are feeling any ill-effects as a result of their malevolence.

It has been suggested that a curse, or hex, can be effective only if the recipient knows of the curse – so that the awareness creates a self-fulfilling prophecy. When you know you have been cursed, you may panic and so you crash the car or lose your credit cards and it seems the curse is working. This makes you even more anxious, so you attract more bad luck and so the cycle goes on ad infinitum – or at least it will, until you take steps to reverse the bad vibes and restore good luck and well-being. However, other people disagree with this proposition, and say that secret malevolence can also affect you. Even if this is true, you will almost certainly be alerted by your unease. In either case, once you are aware of the problem, you can resort to the rituals that will ensure that curses and unconscious bad feelings alike will find, satisfyingly, their own way home to the sender.

When I was under attack, I experienced insomnia, panic attacks, headaches, nausea and a sense of anxiety that made me clumsy, accident-prone and suffering from a spate of minor illnesses that seemed to linger, leaving me permanently exhausted yet enervated. In the case of the love rival, I do not think she was deliberately attacking me psychically but she was certainly obsessed by my existence and constantly questioned my husband about me, and bad-mouthed me. I was made properly aware of the source of the malevolence when she telephoned me with a torrent of verbal abuse, but the psychological and psychic aspects were so entwined that I found it hard to deal with the situation.

A kind, wise medium sent me a blessed cross to put under my pillow and offered prayers on my behalf and taught me various methods of cutting the connection and creating protective barriers to prevent further attacks affecting me. Another dear friend, a white witch, placed a binding spell on my attacker and as I tackled the earthly problems – an essential factor in clearing away the personal negative emotions on which psychic attack can feed – I began to feel any psychic hold diminishing.

In the second case I experienced, the would-be-author's friend telephoned me to inform me that her friend was sending me black balls of negative energy and asked if I was feeling ill or exhausted. I was, but whether the knowledge of the curse then magnified my condition is hard to identify.

This time, I bought two crystal pendants to wear round my neck, an amethyst for calm and a clear crystal quartz to attract positive, healing energies to me. And since I knew the name and location of my enemy, I also returned the curses, visualising them as a parcel I was wrapping up and returning to sender intact and with nothing added. Ironically, had the woman herself phoned me I would have been glad to offer suggestions to help her launch her own career, as I have done many times for other writers.

Although it is sometimes argued that by sending back negativity to its source, you are inflaming the situation and provoking more attacks, it is probably a better mode of action than acceptance, which may only encourage your tormentor further.

On occasions when I have been cursed by gypsies (not true Romanies), for example when I would not buy their sprigs of rosemary or lavender for their extortionately high prices, I have bounced the curse back to its sender. I have described a method using mirrors later in this chapter. Once, in Covent Garden in London, a gypsy muttered curses after me and as I walked away I felt a physical force, like a wall of steel, heading towards me. I quickly said, 'You can have that back', and there was a sound like metal striking something and rebounding. To my surprise, as I turned, I saw her sitting on the ground.

Because this is such a sensitive area, it is important to deal only with your own negativity and that of close family or friends. A woman I knew, who went round exorcising buildings, ended up with a very nasty case of spirit attack herself. If in doubt, contact your local Spiritualist church or a sympathetic priest for help.

Methods of repelling psychic attack

In this section, I will describe some simple but potent methods of repelling malevolence or hostility. These can be used if a work colleague or family member is making your life unbearable, remembering that this is extraordinary, rather than general psychic protection.

These rituals may also be helpful against a stalker, an anonymous caller or 'poison pen' writer whose identity is unknown. Unless you are 100 per cent certain of the identity of the anonymous assailant, it is better not to name a person even if you have strong suspicions. It would be unfair to send back negativity to the wrong source. The rituals are also potent against actual curses and against poltergeist attack.

A *cutting and binding ritual against psychic attack*

If you simply bind a person, known or unknown, from harming you or someone you love, your attacker may still have their energies tangled with yours and so you may not feel free. The following ritual can be used in addition to ongoing personal psychic self-defence.

- Surround yourself with a circle of protective incense or scented candles, for example pine, eucalyptus, cypress, lemon, rosemary or tea-tree.

- Make a featureless image in clay (if possible, use clay that you have found on a beach or hillside or that comes from a natural source) to represent your attacker.

- As you work, endow the figure with positive energies, using a chant such as:

    Love, light and loveliness flow, kindness, wisdom, joy to know.

- Loop three pieces of red wool around the figure and around three fingers of your left hand, keeping the image on the table.

- Cut the loops one by one from your fingers, saying:

    Ties that bind, cut, unwind,
    Free from negativity.

- Tie the three pieces of wool with nine knots around the image, saying:

    Bind from harm.
    Peaceful calm,
    Think not of me,
    Nor to see, not to send,
    Anger end.

- Wrap the image in soft pink wool or white cotton wool and place it in a small dark box.

- Bury it in a very deep hole beneath a healing tree, such as an ash or rowan, away from your home, if possible in a deserted place. Let the earth absorb the negativity – remember you are burying the harm, not the person.

- Now do something positive to heal the earth, to restore the balance: pick up some litter, plant seeds in a barren place, remove weeds from a choked stream or give a small donation to an endangered species.

When you see the person you believe was attacking you, greet them politely, but avoid eye contact or personal conversation where possible. If the incidents of attack continue, repeat the ritual as many times as necessary, making the loops on your fingers looser and the knots tighter.

Protection with mirrors

Mirrors are used in both Eastern and Western spirituality to repel negativity. Hathor, the Egyptian goddess of love, music and dancing and protectress of women, was once entrusted with the sacred eye of Ra, the Sun God, through which she could see all things. She carried a shield that could reflect back all things in their true light. From her shield, she fashioned the first magic mirror. One side was endowed with the power of Ra's eye to see everything, no matter how distant in miles or how far into the future. The other side showed the gazer in his or her true light and only a brave person could look at it without flinching. Therefore, mirrors became associated with truth and light, especially solar radiance, and assumed a protective as well as divinatory function.

The Pa'kua

For home use, some people use a Chinese *Pa'kua* (also spelt *Pah Kwa* or *Bau-gua*) as an amulet. It is not an indoor device, as it is said to be too powerful – it is usually reflective, with a mirror in the middle.

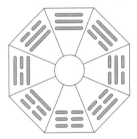

The Pa'kua is placed on gates to drive away negativity and avert misfortune. Sometimes it is placed above the main door, always reflecting outwards. A Pa'kua is based on eight forces that are said to make up the *ch'i*, or life force, that runs through all existence; beginning from the top and going round clockwise, the eight symbols signify Sky, Wind or Wood, Water, Mountain, Earth, Thunder, Fire and Lake or Marsh.

Instead of a Pa'kua, you may prefer to use a small oval or round unadorned mirror that you can hang indoors, perhaps in your bedroom; it should not face your bed, but be set towards the outside world from where negativity comes. You can also position a small decorative mirror on an office desk or work bench to deter unfriendly visitors and unfair criticism.

A ritual for charging your mirror

You need to charge your mirror with power and protection. To do this, prop your mirror in a garden or on a balcony so that sunlight is shining on it. The best time is at noon on the day of the full moon.

- Surround your mirror with a circle of golden or yellow flowers. Lift the mirror towards the sun and turn the mirror until it is filled with light, then continue to turn it, saying:

    East, south, west, north, dark and evil come not forth,
    Eye of truth, reflect from here, sorrow, envy, hatred, fear.

- Spin your mirror faster and faster and chant faster and faster until you are moving yourself round and round still holding the mirror and you feel yourself filled with golden light.

- Replace the mirror in the circle, saying:

    Solar light,
    In me bright,
    Flame and burn,
    Evil turn.

- At this point, scatter the flowers to the four winds, calling out:

    From its thrall, as I call – darkness, begone.

- If you are the subject of a great deal of negativity, hang charged mirrors facing doors and windows in the four main directions. They will deflect back any curses or hostility, conscious or otherwise, to the sender.

- Place a mirror over the phone table to deter anonymous callers.

- Hang wind chimes, dream catchers and silver and brass bells near entrances and windows to increase your protection.

You should also cleanse your mirror regularly. Use a weak rosemary infusion or pure running water and then polish it with a white silk cloth, first anti-clockwise and then clockwise.

Witch balls

These resemble huge Christmas baubles, traditionally silver, but also in red, blue and green. Used for divination, especially out of doors, like a traditional crystal ball, the reflective surface is highly protective. I first saw them in Burley, in the New Forest in Hampshire, UK, former home of the witch Sybil Leek. However, they are also popular in the United States.

A witch ball is generally suspended from a tree in the garden to move gently in the wind and hold changing images of the greenery and flowers; as it turns, it deflects curses and negativity as they enter the land. Your witch ball can also be suspended on a balcony, in a hallway or near the back door or by a window that looks out on to the street. If possible, ensure a gentle breeze circulates around it.

You can make a witch ball yourself, from any ornamental glass ball, decorating it with silver, gold or green metallic paint; you could even paint a goldfish bowl and place it, upside-down, on a tall rock, a tree stump or a table so that air circulates all round from the four directions, thus offering protection from malice wherever it originates. Modern silver discotheque balls also make excellent witch balls. Charge and cleanse as for a mirror (see page 121), being careful to keep liquid to a minimum. If you make your own, you can silently endow it with secret words of power and love.

A *ritual for sending back pain*

I am including this ritual here because it is the most potent spell I have come across for returning all forms of attack, whether it involves personal malevolence, someone bullying a child, threatening the home, or gossiping spitefully. Again you do not need to know the perpetrator of the evil and even if you do, it may be better not to name them, as this is such a potent ritual and always comes true.

This ritual is especially effective when carried out at the time of the waning moon, or on any moonless light.

- Take nine iron nails and place them in a dark glass bottle with a few sprigs of rosemary, some milk that is beginning to curdle and some very cheap, red wine that has gone sour.

- Put the cork in the bottle and shake it, saying:

> May venom and viciousness be gone,
> Bottle up the evil to me done.

- Purify a sink or drain with a few drops of fenugreek, tea-tree or pine oil, dissolved in warm water with a sprinkling of salt, saying:

> May spite and malice lose their sway,
> Harmful deeds be washed away.

- Shake the bottle well and tip the contents down the drain or sink saying:

> Pain and sorrow go from me,
> I send you back to he or she
> Inflicter of disharmony.
> Wheresover you may be.

- Rinse out the bottle with very hot water and tip any remnants away, washing until the water from the bottle runs clear.

- When the bottle is empty, say:

> I have returned the pain,
> Send it not again.

- Purify the bottle by placing in it a clear crystal quartz and some pure spring water and leaving it in sunlight and starlight for 72 hours. Repeat the ritual as necessary.

A *Viking ritual for protection*

In the section on protective amulets, I gave examples of how the Vikings and Anglo-Saxons carved runes for power and protection. The most protective rune is Thorn, the hammer of Thor, and this defensive ritual is especially powerful against threats of physical violence or attacks on property.

This ritual was traditionally practised using salt and pepper as cleansers (see later), but it seems to work just as well with incense. Sandalwood, oakmoss, clove and sage are all incenses sacred to Thor (and also to Jupiter, the other thunderbolt-wielding god). It is designed to help if you feel under threat or psychic attack, whether from a known or unknown source.

- In the centre of a circle of white paper, draw a circle of touching Thorn runes (see above), with the points extending outwards. Place the paper on a fireproof tray for safety.

- Around the paper, light a circle of Thor incenses (see above), in very narrow containers so that the ash falls on the paper. Allow the incense to burn through, visualising each of your Thorns as made of fire whose collective light encircles you.

- When the incense is burned through, collect the ash in the centre of the paper with a twig. If possible, use a twig from a thorn tree or any other protective wood (see pages 69–72), reciting as you do:

> By the power of Thor, protect me from all who wish
> and would do me harm.

- Draw in the ash with your twig a circle of Thorn runes, again pointing outwards in a circle.

- Fold your paper inwards so that the ash remains in the centre and go to an open place – a balcony will do.

- Open the paper and scatter ash to the north, then the east, south and west, saying:

> By the power of Thor, send protection from the north against all who wish
> and would do me harm.

For each of the other directions, repeat the chant, naming east, south and then west in turn.

- When you have scattered the ash, light a blue candle on a metal tray and burn the paper, seeing as you do so the circle of Thorns encircling you.

- Place this ash in a small blue bag, tied with nine knots, and carry it with you, together with a Thorn rune you have drawn on stone or etched in wood.

Curses and black magic

I have already written about deliberate malevolence. Curses take this malevolence one step further: they are words of malice deliberately directed towards another person, often by magical means, whether by spells or incantations or by sending evil in a symbolic form. Sometimes the curse can come from an embittered relative, or a former friend turned enemy or jealous rival. The process and its effects are no different from the psychic attacks I talked about earlier and in fact, like psychic attackers, the senders of formal curses call up all kinds of trouble for themselves by invoking malevolent spirits to work for them. They usually summon up nothing more fearsome than their own fevered imaginations, but once that negativity is released as a thought form it will cause far more distress to the sender than the recipient.

Not only witches and sorcerers but also ordinary people and even priests have in all cultures, and at all times, inflicted what might be termed deliberate formal psychic attack on enemies. So if you are cursed, especially by some exotically dressed individual in a language you (and maybe he or she!) does not really understand, it may seem really frightening. I know I felt a shiver of terror when cursed by a Gitana, a Spanish gypsy, outside the Alhambra Palace in Granada in southern Spain, because I would not buy her rosemary. I was even more spooked when my bag was stolen outside a pavement café two days later, also in Granada, but that was almost certainly more to do with my own carelessness in putting it down on the floor in an area renowned for thieves. However, the bag contained a Spanish Tarot pack I had just bought and I have the satisfaction of knowing the terror that would have been inflicted on the thieves when they discovered their prize.

Malevolent attack is different from the evil eye, which tends to stem from unconscious envy or jealousy and is much closer to the free-floating hostility that may be released by our enemies as they fume about us or gossip about us in our absence.

How curses work

At the beginning of this chapter, I touched on a crucial question: is a curse more effective or indeed only possible if the victim knows of it, thereby activating a self-fulfilling prophecy or making a psychic connection? This certainly seems to explain the effects of some curses. For example, in diverse parts of the world – Africa, Malaysia and Australia – there is a tradition of pointing. A witch doctor may point a bone or dagger at a victim, who, realising he or she is cursed, loses the will to live. Victims may even be shunned by their fellow tribespeople.

There is evidence too that people said to have been struck down by a curse imposed by those who sought in centuries past to protect their tombs from grave robbers would have known of the curse mythology surrounding ancient tombs. Take the much-documented case of the tomb of Tutankhamun which is said to be protected by a curse upon all who opened it, as were other ancient tombs throughout Egypt and Asia. The Earl of Carnarvon and Howard Carter were the first to enter Tutankhamun's burial chamber in 1922 and found its treasures undisturbed by earlier grave robbers. Legend has it that in an antechamber they found an inscribed tablet which read: *Death Shall Come on Swift Wings to Him who Disturbs the Peace of the King.* Whether or not this was true, six of the seven people present at the opening of the tomb met strange deaths within a relatively short time.

However, such curses may have a more natural explanation. In the case of the 'pointing', the element of belief of the victim would appear to be a crucial part of the curse. There may also be an even more scientific explanation. In the case of Tutankhamun's tomb, in 1999, a German microbiologist, Gotthard Kramer, from the University of Leipzig, suggested that potentially dangerous mould spores that had survived in the tomb for thousands of years may have been released – and so those who opened ancient tombs activated what was a natural, rather than a magical curse.

Ways of using curses

The most common method of cursing a person in black magic involves using a representation of the victim – for example, an effigy created from the melted wax of a black candles – and sticking pins in it. Curse images were used from early times in India, Persia, Ancient Egypt, Africa and Europe and the practice continues in parts of Africa, India, the Middle East, the West Indies and Central and South America today.

Dolls were also made from clay, wood or cloth. An effigy would be painted or embroidered to resemble the victim, and if possible some physical part of the victim, such as hair clippings, nail parings or even pubic hair, was attached to the doll. The doll was then harmed or destroyed; in the case of a faithless lover, the heart and genital area would be pierced with a pin. The intention was to transfer the pain to the victim, by a process of contagious magic.

Animal or human hearts and eggs were buried close to the victim's home, so that as they decayed, it was intended, so would be the cursed person.

Babylonian demon bowls
In Iran and Iraq, inscribed earthenware bowls, known as Babylonian demon bowls, dating back as early as the sixth century, have been found buried face downwards or sometimes stuck together with pitch; written around the rim were magical formulae and images of demons, and inside the bowls were eggshells or even human skull bones. They were placed in the corners of rooms and used to trap demons who might harm the family and home. However, literature suggests that sometimes the bowls were used to trap demons that were then released against enemies.

Lead wishing tablets
Another form of protective magic that overlapped with and developed into active curse magic was the use of lead wishing tablets. They were called *katadesmoi* in Ancient Greece and *defixiones* in Latin. Curse tablets that have been recovered from the Roman baths at Bath in Avon show the name of a wrongdoer or an unknown thief or murderer and his or her evil deeds inscribed on the lead. Sometimes a magical binding ritual guarded against further evil deeds and the tablet was then cast into the waters. What was not realised was that the tablets carried another curse, in that over time they dissolved slightly, releasing poison into the water.

Ritual and the Devil

Where magic and spirituality is concerned, even in the modern world the Devil, chief of the fallen hosts, still brings out an almost superstitious dread in popular consciousness. This is so even among some who profess no formal religion. He is personified in the Judeo-Christian image of the Devil card in the Tarot that has undeservedly contributed towards the Tarot's reputation as the Terror Cards.

This association between the paranormal and the Devil still underpins both official and popular prejudice against psychic development and healing practices. Witchcraft has through the ages also been unfairly associated with Satanic worship, and many innocent men and women confessed under torture to consorting with the Devil in the form of a goat, during the witch burnings that continued throughout Europe and Scandinavia for three centuries or more from medieval times. The vast majority of those who were practising witchcraft were not worshipping the Devil, but following the old nature religions that continued in remote places even until the nineteenth century. The Goat God was the descendant of the Shamanic horned figure who appeared on cave walls thousands of years ago and is associated with the Horned God, consort of the Earth Mother.

Charlatans and how to avoid them

Just as there was in past times a very small but dangerous minority of demon worshippers and witches who followed black magic, nowadays there are groups who use the name of magic as an excuse for depravity, paedophilia and a lust for personal power. Happily, you are unlikely to encounter dark forces if you maintain the same natural caution towards those who practise magic as you would any other unknown organisation. However, I would recommend that you avoid getting involved with groups who encourage the consumption of drugs and excessive alcohol or sexual practices that are deviant as part of what is claimed to be a religious ceremony.

It is possible that you may meet someone who seems inexplicably strange to you; they may try to practise hypnotism on you, or immediately invite you to a join a coven; or they may ask for money to rid you of your enemies. If this happens, apply the same caution you would whenever you encounter strangers in other situations. This caution itself protects those genuinely interested in magic from the more dubious practices of undesirable people masquerading under the guise of witchcraft. In fact, genuine Wiccan groups (followers of the religious cult of modern witchcraft) are unlikely to approach you in such a way: they are expert at shielding themselves from curious teenagers or adults eager for what they imagine to be an opportunity for free love and a good time.

Answering adverts in the paper to join magic groups or covens can be risky; you should always arrange to meet people you do not know in a public place and even then offer no personal information. I myself have come across people claiming to be Wiccans who instantly steer the conversation round to weird sexual practices and sexual demons. This is the time to back off quickly, for no genuine white witch would behave in this way.

Beware also of strangers or acquaintances who regale you with supposed Wiccan practices or offer to do spells for you, usually for money, or clairvoyants and gurus who claim you have been cursed and offer to remove the curses or reverse the bad luck – but always for a fee.

If you are afraid, there are several sources of help available to you. You can contact a sympathetic priest (every diocese has an expert in the paranormal, so if someone seems unsympathetic ask for more expert help); or a medium (through a Spiritualist church); or a healer (again, through an accredited organisation); or a Wiccan priest or priestess, through a reputable pagan organisation (see the chapter on Useful Contacts, pages 182–7, for reliable sources of help). An amateur exorcist or someone claiming to be a medium can do more harm than good and may sometimes actually convince people they are being haunted when they are not.

Above all, keep a sense of perspective and common sense. A person who suddenly appears and curses you is most likely to be mentally ill and more deserving of pity than fear.

Demonic attack in the modern world

In medieval times, it was believed that there were evil spirits, called *Incubi*, sexual demons who preyed on women, and *Saccubi*, who attacked men. Today, a minority of adolescent girls and young women, and sometimes adolescent boys, perhaps far more than officially admit to such experiences, are plagued by the twenty-first-century equivalent of these demons. The person concerned may wake to find that they are being crushed by a weight that prevents movement and feel as if they are being sexually attacked by an invisible force. Generally, there is only one such experience, but the effects may remain for months. Some people in the modern world have compared this experience with accounts of the phenomenon of alien abduction, especially those given by young women.

Jill, now a married woman in her thirties, gave the following account of her experience with one of these demons:

'When I was 13 or 14, I started to have a dream about an upside-down cross. We weren't a religious family and never went to church. I was horrified to be told by my friends that it was to do with the Devil. Not long after I had an awful vision of the Devil. He had huge horns like a ram and a horrible face. His face was dark and half-ram, half-human. I think I said a prayer. I felt a physical force. He was trying to crush me. I was absolutely terrified. It lasted 10 or 15 seconds, I suppose, but it was like eternity.'

My own view is that many of these experiences partly originate in the inner conflicts about power and sexuality that can be especially problematic for sensitive women whose families will not talk about such matters. Sometimes, the 'demon' can be linked to unresolved childhood conflict.

However, this is not the whole answer and I know that some clergymen disagree with me and see these entirely as demonic attacks. Often the young person does have a fascination with the darker side of the para-normal and may even have played with a ouija board; for this reason I think it is important that the psychic world should not be hidden, but discussed openly with teenagers, as we do the subjects of sex, drugs and alcohol, so they are not left alone with their fears.

If there is more than one such incident, the problem will usually cease if the sufferer has the bedroom blessed or performs a salt and water ritual. A protective salt ritual is described later in this chapter (see page 133) and the rituals in the chapter on Everyday Psychic Self-defence (see page 138) may also help in making night-time less threatening to those plagued by night terrors of any form. But the greatest protection is the ability of the victim to talk freely to someone who is sympathetic; the listener must not dismiss the experiences as pure imagination, but will help to move the issue into the wider context of the person's whole life and fears.

Poltergeists and psychokinetic energy

Another paranormal phenomenon associated with evil is the poltergeist. One modern theory cites the cause of poltergeist activity as emanating from a living member of the household, usually an adolescent, and especially female. Young women in their early twenties may unconsciously release repressed anger or anxiety. This stress, which may be caused by family or the emotional disturbances of awakening sexuality, manifests itself in the form of psychokinetic energy (the force whereby the mind causes objects to move). Sometimes two people may seem to be the agent for poltergeist activity, especially if there is an emotionally or sexually charged relationship between them. It is very difficult to distinguish in such cases between the psychic and the psychological, or to tell the paranormal from the earthly.

It is frequently noticeable that, once the family member who is generating the negativity in the younger person (perhaps a violent or over-critical parent or a quarrelsome spouse) leaves the home, and the practical as well as the spiritual needs of the sufferer are provided for by sympathetic outsiders, the phenomenon ceases to exist. In most cases, open discussion of problems at home and the defusing of negative anger before bedtime, as well as regular psychic domestic cleansing and rituals to shed personal negativity (described in earlier chapters) will prevent free-floating and relatively common psychokinetic energies from building up into a full-scale poltergeist onslaught.

Unfriendly ghosts

If there is no particular tension in your home and no obvious source of the poltergeist activity, the haunting may be caused by a restless ghost or the trapped energies of a deceased person who experienced tragedy in the affected place. Some rooms always seems dark, even on the sunniest day; animals may be reluctant to enter them or may stare at a particular corner; and certain areas may always feel freezing cold, even if they are next to a radiator. If you hold a pendulum over these spots, it may spiral anti-clockwise but instead of feeling that this is caused by the negative Earth energies that can also cause rooms to feel hostile, you may build up in your mind's eye, or briefly externally, an image of your resident ghost. What is more, if you feel that you are being watched or detect shadows out of the corner of your eye or hear the growling or howling of animals where none exists, then again a ghost may be a likely explanation. Even modern houses can be haunted by phantoms from the land on which they are built. A remarkable number of today's Abbey Closes and Monastery Ways on housing estates have monks and nuns wandering around.

If the ghost seems friendly, then it may well be a former inhabitant of the house or a deceased relative who may announce their presence with the scent of a favourite perfume or tobacco that will be most noticeable on family anniversaries. Children often detect these ghosts and if they are not worried, neither should you be. But an apparition that bangs and crashes in the night, frightening the children and the animals, is definitely one house guest too many. For the most part, they are not malevolent, just plain miserable, but that is no consolation if it is 2am and the pots and pans are rattling on the stove.

The following experience occurred one Easter while I was on holiday in Spain, and suggests one method, using scented candles and opening doors and windows, of encouraging your phantom to move on.

I had arrived with my family in Nerja in Andalucia, hoping for a break from the paranormal. Nevertheless, I took along my pendulum and my husband John took his two metal angle rods, an alternative dowsing device.

To our surprise, the hotel management gave us not the apartment we had expected but La Granda Casa, a white-washed villa overlooking the sea. On the first night, the noises began: I heard footsteps outside my bedroom, but when I opened the door to see which child was awake, all of them were asleep, and in the morning they also complained about footsteps. My husband's electronic diary started to ring at irregular intervals and was heard in the night by our older son Jack, though on examination it appeared to be switched off.

On the second night, the toilet flushed every few minutes and the bath taps turned on and off right through the night. We all separately heard voices and on the third night I had a troubling dream of a dark, faceless figure who could not speak. The next day, my daughter Miranda claimed to have seen me on the open staircase at a time I was not in the house. Strangest of all was that although most Spanish properties have bars across downstairs doors and windows to deter intruders, this house was a veritable prison, with bars at every door and window, some of which were painted over and had obviously never opened. The door gates automatically slammed locked from the inside and could only be opened with a key, effectively trapping any occupants inside, which I considered to be a fire hazard.

Using a pendulum, I located the same point on each of three floors, including the cellar, which had a barred room containing old dusty furniture; at each of these points, the pendulum swung strongly in an anti-clockwise direction. John then walked around the house using his two metal rods that he held vertically parallel in front of him. They suddenly crossed over at precisely the same points at which my pendulum had identified the negative energies.

One of these points was in the corridor where we had heard the footsteps, directly outside the bathroom. The energies here were whirling round like a fish trapped in reeds, making the pendulum vibrate quite painfully, especially outside the bathroom, so I turned the pendulum in an anti-clockwise direction over the negative eddies, to clear the blockage. Next, I found a positive path, where the crystal pendulum swung clockwise, along which the presence wanted to move, beginning from the strongest negative spot outside the bathroom. The path went down the staircase, pausing at the place where Miranda had seen the figure, to the ground floor door and through the gate, which we had struggled to unbar and open, leading to the terrace overlooking the sea.

We eventually managed to open all the doors in the house, except for one, and we left the barred gates pushed back when we were close to the house. We also lit scented candles each night, pine and lemon for cleansing and rose and lavender for love and acceptance and carried them around all the places we had detected the negative energies and along the subsequent path to freedom.

The atmosphere lightened and by the fifth day the pendulum was showing no response anywhere in the house. Only on the last night were there noises, but this was happy singing. Had the ghost become locked into the house or were the bars an unsuccessful attempt by the absent owner to keep the phantom out? I'm afraid I do not have the answers: it did not seem right to try to unravel the identity of the ghost since we were only visitors and the presence was perhaps some unresolved issue in the owner's past.

Salt

Of all substances, salt has in all ages and cultures been used to give protection against psychic attack of all types, whether from mortal or paranormal source. Salt rituals are among the oldest forms of magic, and salt has always been central to religious and magical practices because it was the one absolutely pure substance. It was regarded as precious because it was the main preservative of food through the long winter months for early settlers around the globe.

The Westernised name comes from Salus, Roman goddess of health, whom the Greeks called Hygeia. The Greeks and Romans mixed salt with their sacrificial cakes and threw salt on sacrificial fires. Salt was also used in ceremonies of sacrifice by the Jews. In later Christian belief, salt and water were considered potent in restoring health to the body and in the exorcism of evil spirits.

The preservative quality of salt endowed it with religious symbolism of purity and incorruptibility. In earlier times, salt was placed in coffins as protection against the Devil. In lands populated by the Celts, a plate containing a pinch of salt and a pinch of earth was laid upon the breast of the newly deceased to indicate the mortal corruptible body and the immortal, incorruptible soul. Salt was also used with holy water to ward off evil and increase physical strength as well as powers of fertility. It is still used in the preparation of holy water.

Salt may also be effective in moving on ghosts. However, if the ghost seems especially unfriendly towards you, rather than just sad, an experienced medium will be able to explain the presence and help him or her to depart in peace.

In magic, salt was traditionally scattered around thresholds and in protective circles against all evil influences. Spilled salt would be cast over the left shoulder into the eye of the Devil or of evil spirits who were believed from Roman times onwards to lurk on the left side (our word 'sinister' is in fact derived directly from the Latin for left, *sinister*). The belief in spilling salt came from the idea that accidentally tipping such a sacred substance would invite retribution. In Leonardo da Vinci's painting *The Last Supper*, the upturned salt cellar reflects the belief that such an action represented a breaking of trust and friendship.

Modern ritual no longer concentrates primarily on casting out demons or dark spirits, and many modern practitioners feel that the idea of casting out ghosts is very negative, since a spirit may be unhappy or confused rather than evil. Also the business of banishing and rescuing spirits is an area that I consider is best left to priests or experienced mediums.

Wiccans (followers of modern witchcraft) do not believe in evil spirits per se, but rather in redirecting an energy that may be manifest as negativity. The following rituals will bring light and healing to any paranormal presences in your home or workplace, so that they will either become less noisy or intrusive or naturally move on. The salt rituals are also good for removing earthly negativity from your home and for preventing malevolence of all kinds, whether bad feelings against you, free-floating malice or actual curses, from entering your home.

A *simple protective salt ritual*

This can be used either for a particular room or a whole flat or house.

- Mix a few pinches of sea salt in a crystal dish with pure spring water, or rainwater that has not touched the ground, or sacred water from a holy well.

- Sprinkle a few drops of salt water in the four corners of the room and place a small outward-facing mirror or hang a clear quartz crystal at each window to reflect back negative feelings coming from outside. If you want to protect the whole house, mix a larger quantity of salt water in a larger metal or unglazed pottery bowl.

- As you sprinkle the water, say:

    By salt and water, purify this home, bless all who dwell therein and may only light and love remain.

This blessing should be used if you sense a ghost rather than just general negativity.

- Sprinkle the salt water in a clockwise circle around the area where you feel the presence most strongly, saying;

    Friend, if it be right, depart in peace or remain as guardian and benign protector of all who share this sacred space with you.

- You can then burn scented candles in lemon, pine, lavender and rose – or any other cleansing and peace-enhancing fragrances (see Psychic Protection in Nature, page 67). Incense is good as well.

- Then open all the doors and windows and let in the light energy and if it is right, the phantom should have an easy path outwards.

In their ceremony for a departed member, the Wiccans sometimes say that he or she is always welcome in the circle. Certainly, if I were a ghost, I would be more inclined to oblige by departing if the mortal were being polite, rather than cursing me in Latin and burning foul-smelling substances.

A *more complex salt ritual for protection*

This ritual may be used if the previous ritual did not seem to work or was only effective temporarily, or if you are waking with inexplicable night terrors, and feel under attack, whether from a paranormal source or earthly malice. Because salt represents the Earth element, it grounds your room in calm, benign influences. This is a more potent form of the cleansing ritual with herb infusions described in the chapter on Domestic Protection (see page 24). It may also work in the case of a minor haunting or feeling of unease.

- Place a small quantity of sea salt or a coarse-grained salt in a small dish on a table in the centre of the room.

- Now bless each room in turn: if the whole house is affected, begin at the front door, then goes upstairs and work in each room, finally coming downstairs and ending at the back door. If there is a basement or cellar, bless that before doing the downstairs and cleanse the attics first. In each affected room, carry out all the following stages, saying first:

> *Salt of the Earth, heal and protect all who dwell here,*
> *living and departed.*

- Pass over the dish a lighted incense stick or oil burner with a protective fragrance such as pine, lemon or peppermint; this Air element will blow away negativity. As you do so, say:

> *Fragrance of the Air, bless and release from sorrow all who dwell here,*
> *living and dead.*

- Pass next a lighted candle of protective pink or purple over the salt for the Fire element. See the light spreading outwardly in spirals and say:

> *Flame of fire, purge all darkness, leaving only light and radiance in*
> *all who dwell here, living and departed.*

- Blow out the candle, sending the light to every corner of the room.

- Finally, sprinkle a few drops of rose water or any floral oil, such as geranium or jasmine, for the Water element and let the healing waters restore love and harmony to the room and say:

> *Waters, gentle and still, bring love and harmony to every corner of my*
> *home and all who dwell therein, living and departed.*

- Once more, circle with salt the place where any paranormal presence haunts, saying:

  Friend, it may be it is time for you to move on. If so, go with our blessing and return a welcome visitor.

- Finally, sprinkle a circle of salt around yourself, saying:

  Let only love and light come within this circle, darkness flee.

- Leave tiny drawstring bags of salt or twists of salt in silver foil in each corner for a few days and you will feel the atmosphere lighten.

The evil eye

Throughout the book there have been references to herbs, crystals and amulets to protect against the 'evil eye'. So what is the evil eye and does it exist or does it belong to the superstitious past?

The first references to the evil eye appear in the cuneiform texts of the Assyro-Babylonians, around 3000 BC. At a later period, Roman men, women and children so feared the eye that they carried phallus-shaped charms (to counter the oval female shape of the eye) in gold, silver and bronze as antidotes.

Even today, in the Middle East, Italy and Spain, Central America and Mexico, belief in the evil eye remains strong, especially in remote areas, and blue-eyed people, who are rare among the indigenous people, are especially under suspicion. Blue eyes are, of course, relatively rare in adults in some peoples – 'a blue-eyed boy', an expression for someone who is unfairly favoured, comes from the same root thoughts.

The evil eye is believed to operate primarily on an unconscious level, transmitting negativity to another person, not as a deliberate curse, but through envy or jealousy. It may provoke resentment towards a person considered as fortunate, or intense desire to possess an artefact belonging to another.

This desire, whether focused on property, wealth, health or fertility, was traditionally believed particularly to affect infants and children because they were vulnerable and open to psychic influences. In times when hygiene was poor and infant mortality high, it was used to explain why an infant might suddenly fail to thrive or an animal grow sick.

The evil eye could also, it was said, be cast upon grazing animals, fruit trees and crops. It was claimed that houses burst into flames and ploughs or farm machinery might break, as a result of a covetous eye being cast on them. Ironically the influence was believed to be passed on through overt praise of, for example, a pretty or healthy child, a fine animal or an orchard with trees in blossom, and so, in more superstitious times and places, even a genuine compliment was feared. So a bad harvest, a sick child or a blighted fruit crop might unfairly be blamed on a stranger or someone who appeared different from the community and had tried to be friendly by admiring a newborn infant or a well-tended garden.

Because belief in the evil eye was relatively widespread and its potency did not seem to depend on the perpetrator possessing special psychic powers, fears of psychic attack were quite common. Therefore anyone genuinely wanting to admire an infant or animal would afterwards spit or touch the infant to remove the influence of the evil eye.

If this was not done, the mother or owner would either offer a prayer or moderate the praise by pointing out a defect in the infant or coveted object. A child might even be smeared with dirt before being taken out in public and bells were hung from cradles and prams for the same reason. Even in my own childhood in the 1950s, in an industrial town in England, praise was not something that was welcomed, as people – including my mother – would say it brought bad luck.

If a child or animal became sick, or household accidents occurred, or crops became blighted, the evil eye was in earlier times a prime suspect, along with deliberate witchcraft. Water, oils or other liquids were used both for detection and as a remedy, since it was thought that the evil eye caused the natural fluids that sustained life to dry up. In Eastern Europe, for example, charcoal, coal, or burnt match heads were dropped into a bowl of water. If they floated, it was said the evil eye had been cast. A local wise woman would be sought who knew the secret words to take away the influence – and these formulae were passed down through the matriarchs of large families and communities. Holy water would sometimes be sprinkled at the same time on a victim, whether it was a human, an animal or even blighted trees or crops.

In Italy, olive oil was dripped into water, a single drop at a time, while the matriarch recited her secret mantras. If the drops formed an eye, prayers would be said over the victim while oil was continuously dripped until a series of shapes appeared instead of the eye formation. In Mexico, an egg was rolled across the supposed victim's body and then cracked to see if an eye formed in the yolk. A cross was drawn on the forehead with the egg while incantations were made. Afterwards the eggs were thrown away in a shady place or buried to prevent a second attack. Holy water was also sprinkled over the victim.

Charms against the evil eye

Carrying charms, especially eye charms – for example the Eye of Horus, the Egyptian Sun God, (see page 50) – were regarded as a potent method of repelling attack, the idea being that the more powerful eye, for example that of Horus, would be stronger than the evil glance. From Assyrian times, camels were traditionally protected by wearing a stone with a hole around their necks and horses in many cultures had blue beads, sometimes specially made of turquoise, in their manes and bridles (see Protective Amulets, Talismans and Charms, page 36).

In Greece and Turkey, a blue glass eye charm was said to mirror back the evil eye and thus confound it. Blue was the antidote for the gaze of the blue-eyed stranger (see page 135). In India, cord charms from which hang blue beads are still worn by newborn babies. Once the cord breaks, the child is thought old enough to resist attack.

The most common protective symbols in India, Israel and Arab lands is an engraved eye within a palm, covered with magical symbols, that has become Christianised as the hand of God or manopoderosa.

A scientific view of the evil eye

Modern researchers are moving away from the physical aspect of 'evilling' to an awareness that negative feelings could be carried by telepathy when a person spontaneously visualises a cause of envy or resentment. At the same time scientific research is discovering that people are aware when they are being stared at even if they cannot see the person who is looking at them. The Cambridge biologist, Dr Rupert Sheldrake, is carrying out ongoing research into this subject and it would seem from the results over several years that minds can reach out and affect those they are thinking about, albeit benignly, in experiments.

This would then confirm that the eye charms are potent amulets against even distant malevolence directed your way. Often it seems that when science tries to explain superstition in its own terms, it serves only to confirm the folk wisdom of centuries in psychological as well as psychic terms.

EIGHT

Everyday Psychic Self-defence

As I said in the introduction to this book, psychic protection is as natural as putting on work clothes in the morning and checking that your mobile phone is charged and that you have your ticket and money for the day. If you prepare in advance, you arrive unhurried and do not leave yourself vulnerable, accident-prone and panicking if there are delays or problems on your journey. Equally, when you return in the evening, you may have a bath and change your clothes and feel the tensions flowing away.

These routine actions create a barrier against the outside world and this is the purpose of good psychic self-defence: to mark and strengthen the boundaries between you and the outside world. In the morning you are increasing positive energies to resist stress and in the evening you are slowing down the pace to shed the day and allow a calmer mood to predominate. If you are a shift-worker, you can modify the times you carry out these little rituals, to fit in with your life.

Our earthly and psychic actions are linked. If you are permanently feeling rushed and late or you live in clutter and suffer constant demands on your time even when you are supposed to be relaxing, then it is easier for negative energies to accumulate (see the chapter on Domestic Protection, page 24). The workaholic needs really strong psychic self-defence – and maybe a re-ordering of worldly priorities.

Creating your protected, connected self

Few of us in the modern world do have the time or space to withdraw for long periods to re-establish the still, calm centre that enables us to interact with others without being overwhelmed or absorbing negativity, whether it is intentional or free-floating. But there are various steps that we can take even in the busiest schedule to ensure that we are not dissipating our own energies or making ourselves vulnerable to psychic vampirism in others. The following stages to inner harmony can be practised either separately or as a sequence. None of them takes more than a minute or two.

Grounding

Although this process sounds very mysterious and complex, it is in fact, no different from connecting an earth wire in an electric appliance. Humans and animals are naturally connected to the Earth, but this link can get clogged up or even forgotten, especially if you live or work in a tower block or spend a lot of time with high-tech equipment, or travel a great deal, especially at peak times on crowded roads or other busy modes of transport. I mentioned this concept briefly in the first chapter.

The simplest way to ground, or earth, yourself is to stand barefoot on grass or soil. Raise your hands above your head while breathing in, then extend your fingers and slowly lower them towards the earth while breathing out, allowing all the negative energies to drain away.

If you cannot go out of doors, keep a living plant with two dark-coloured crystals in it. Very gently touch the plant, close your eyes and allow what the twelfth-century mystic Hildegard von Bingen called the 'greening process' to reconnect you with the soil.

You should try to ground yourself whenever you feel anxious, jittery or unable to concentrate, or after psychic work. Kneading dough or shaping clay is another way of reconnecting with basic Earth energies and if you make something useful like a loaf or a pot designed to hold things, you can transform free-floating energies into a rooted form.

Whenever possible, go for a walk by yourself or with a friend or family member; choose someone who will not ceaselessly chatter or analyse your relationship or career or family problems. Allow the sensations of the world around you to replace troubling thoughts; concentrate on fragrances, sounds, colours, the taste of salt by the sea or spices in a market. Feel the movement of your feet and absorb the impressions. If you can walk across grassland, hills or sand, the reconnection is more easily made and even urgent anxieties will recede, giving your body and mind time to be restored.

When I walk along the beach near my caravan, I sometimes reflect that many of the worries that were so pressing this time last year never materialised. And that worrying about those that did happen had only increased my own inability to respond to crises. The battles I fought many times in my head were no easier in actuality for my having rehearsed them so many times; but walking weekend after weekend along the wet sand or over the cliffs did help me to feel grounded instead of lost in mists of anxiety.

Centring

This is the logical progression that follows on from grounding. It is very effective if you are receiving impressions from many different sources, conflicting demands on your time and energies, or if you feel that you are being drained of energy. As I have said before, some psychic vampires are not malevolent at all, they merely have a lot of problems and an inability to accept responsibility for their own lives or to seek positive solutions. Children and sick or lonely relatives and friends can also drain us of our natural reserves of strength. Sometimes you cannot shield yourself from them as you need to give out loving energies, and then you do need to centre yourself, so that you do not become so sympathetic or concerned that your own peace of mind and ability to cope are destroyed.

Even in the most positive relationship you may need to feel in your own mind that you are yourself, a separate individual. If you are centred, you are focused and you can concentrate on whatever matter you have in hand, or simply switch off from external pressures and allow your natural restorative energies to come into operation.

Hold your arms by your sides and visualise all the energies that are not yours leaving your body. At the same time, visualise all the energies that are yours but have been scattered returning and forming a circle of light in the centre of your head parallel to your brow chakra, your psychic third eye.

Severing the connection with negativity

The clutter in our minds tends to be of three kinds: obligations we must meet urgently; those that could wait but instead buzz around; and free-floating tension that can be related to our daily routine, events of the past and worries about the future. Some clearly cannot be permanently set aside, but it is important to clear your mind of clutter if it is to be centred and not constantly pulled in different directions. The following ritual is very good for creating the separate space that is necessary for creative and positive spiritual evolution.

- Take symbols of the people around you that drain or dissipate your energies, e.g. angry faxes, print-outs of troublesome e-mails, nasty work memos, shopping lists handed to you by other people ('When you've got a moment…'), requests from children's schools for funds, anything that makes you angry or anxious. If you do not have actual symbols, write a few words that represent the worry on a piece of paper.

- Place the symbols in a box without a lid, and bind the box with red wool, tied with nine red knots, saying:

> Bind and wind nine times through
> Obligations overdue,
> Worries needlessly renewed.

- Cut through the knots, saying:

> Ties so binding,
> Guilt unwinding,
> Freedom finding.

- Finally, light a single, big, white candle and then from it a smaller candle to represent you, separate from all the demands, but still connected in love to those around you, saying:

> Centred in myself alone,
> Troubling thoughts, now begone.

- Blow out the candles and send light to the centre of your mind, to illuminate, focus and renew your unique self.

- Now, without hesitation or anxiety, remove from the box those responsibilities you must deal with instantly. Surround them with already budding greenery.

- Leave in the box the matters you must take up at a future date but which cannot be helped by worrying now. Surround this box with seedlings or small plants that will grow in the near future.

- Finally, take another dark box and put in it the really insoluble matters – those that might happen but which you can do little about, and all the impossible things that other people have demanded and which have been draining or unfruitful.

- Add to these dead leaves and petals and put a lid on the box. Bury this box with the words:

> It is gone, it is done.

You should now have the space in your head to centre your thoughts.

Stilling the mind

If you do not sense any direct hostility around you, all you need to do after you have grounded yourself, and removed all unnecessary mental clutter, is to still your mind so that it can regenerate and work creatively.

The most successful instant method I have encountered is to picture a sky full of stars and watch them going out one by one until you are enclosed in a velvet blackness. Another method is to visualise sitting on an empty train; the train slows down and suddenly stops in the middle of the countryside and gradually all sound and motion ceases. Alternatively (but only if you enjoy flying), imagine yourself in the state of being alone in a plane, flying though cotton wool clouds; the strain of getting to the airport recedes and the arrival is hours away. Whatever your chosen scenario, relax and sink into the stillness around you.

If you have more time, you can relax your body and concentrate on slow, steady breathing, while focusing on a single flower or repeating a word or phrase. Gentle rainforest music or the sound of oceans can also help the process.

When thoughts intrude, sit them gently on an imaginary ferris wheel and let them ascend into the sky, or tie them to balloons and release them to rise gently in the breeze; or set them on water lilies and let them float away downstream. In *The Four Quartets*, TS Eliot called this the 'still point of the turning world'.

When you have established your own method of stilling your mind – and these are limited only by your imagination – create an instant short-cut to your 'still point', so that you can literally throw a switch and withdraw to it whenever you need to. This can be when you are standing on a crowded commuter train, or embroiled in the middle of an office dispute, a never-ending tale of woe from friend or neighbour, or a domestic argument when you can feel your temper boiling.

You may even see this mechanism as a switch activated by an imperceptible click of your fingers or touching your psychic eye (this is situated in the centre of your forehead, just above your physical eyes) and this alone can be a very powerful method of psychic self-defence.

Shielding

In the first chapter I suggested a method for shielding yourself from negative influences. But of course there is a variety of reasons why you might like to erect a shield: perhaps to avoid intrusion of your personal space while travelling; or to filter out negative feelings of jealousy, spite or unfair criticism. Later in this chapter I talk about shielding the aura from negative impressions. You may wonder why I do not simply suggest that we keep a regular shield in place and so avoid any problems: the main reason against this is that although you can ask that only positive and higher energies penetrate, you are creating a barrier and, as with all barriers, it will interfere with the flow of energies. So a shielded life would be a restrictive one, in which emotions would be muted and sensory impressions blunted.

We all need a certain amount of challenge in our lives and sometimes what seems an obstacle or unfair criticism may turn out to be the spur we need to transform ourselves and to change a situation for the better. Equally, if a friend or loved one is in emotional pain or a stranger needs kindness, we do need to share the feelings in order to respond from the heart. If we are to be truly in love, we cannot avoid the fears and anticipation of the early stages, and if the relationship ends we need to experience loss or disappointment in order to move on.

This is not to diminish the importance of psychic shielding. But as you would close your doors and windows against an impending storm, rather than staying indoors all the time, so you can build into the ritual a psychic short-cut to prepare your defences, when the need arises.

Ritual protective prayers and chants

When I was a child, my mother taught me a rhyming prayer, which I believe came from the men who worked in the dark, dangerous tin mines of Cornwall. One of our bedrooms did not have electricity and before entering it, or indeed any dark place, I would spin round, chanting:

> Creatures of darkness, fiend and foe,
> Shades and spectres high and low,
> Father, Son and Holy Ghost,
> Save me from what I fear the most,
> Caverns and mines, boggits wailing,
> Spirits, lost forever calling,
> Protect from what I fear the most,
> Father, Son and Holy Ghost.

At 'Father, Son and Holy Ghost', I would stop, and cross myself. On researching this book, I was fascinated to find several similar protective rituals, from quite separate sources. In all cases, they involved crossing oneself or touching different parts of the body and appealing, in one case, to the various pagan gods and goddesses and in another a godhead who might not be named. I have given what seem to be the most common forms, but I know there are several variations. Indeed, it seems to me that it is quite possible to create your own protective rituals and adapt them to dancing, chanting or more solemn invocations as the situation and your mood demand. I have not used more formal rituals that really belong to the realm of ceremonial magic.

I have simplified the rituals so that you are not using unfamiliar words or the names of deities that perhaps you would not relate to. I believe that reciting invocations that do not have meaning for you personally, however powerful they may be, can lack potency. I have, however, suggested books in which you can find authentic versions (see Further Reading, page 179). If you prefer, you can substitute deities or symbols of divinity or sacredness from any tradition that seems relevant to your own beliefs.

The Wiccan cross

I use this for myself in the unadorned form and allow the deity forms to appear in my mind. The version I give here is a very simple one and can be used by anyone, even if they are unfamilar with mythology. As you speak the words, allow the images of goddesses and gods to form quite naturally in your mind, so that they are personal to you.

Though you are making a cross by touching different parts of your body, additional power is given by turning in a complete circle as you speak. In this way, you draw the protection of the sacred shape of the circle around you.

There is a balance of male and female energies in this ritual, given by incorporating the symbolism of both goddesses and gods. If you prefer, you can focus on either the goddess alone, or the god, in the different forms in which they appear, reflecting the changing seasons that form the circle of the year.

For example, if you wished to follow in your ritual the growth of light from the birth of the Sun God at the midwinter solstice, you could first face the north, then the east, representing the triumph of the god of light over his dark twin at the spring equinox. You would then face south, for the full potency of the Sun God, and finally the west as the god of darkness overcomes his twin, the god of light, at the autumn equinox.

Or you could celebrate the stages of life of the archetypal goddess, beginning by facing the east for the maiden who becomes pregnant in the spring, then south for the mother, west for the wise woman and north for the crone. This particular tradition goes back to Neolithic times, but was especially used by the Celts. Sometimes it is performed as a slow dance and chant. See Further Reading (page 179) for details of different mythologies.

- Standing with your feet together and your arms by your sides, begin by facing east, the direction of the Maiden Goddess who becomes pregnant at the spring equinox. Touch your forehead in the middle of your brow with your right hand and say:

Blessed are you, holy maiden, untouched vessel of new life and fertility. Bless and protect me.

- Turn next to the south, the direction of the horned god of vegetation and animals, consort to the Mother Goddess or one of the gods of the Sun who attains full potency on the summer solstice. Touch either your navel or genitals/womb with your right hand and say:

Blessed are you, father of the herds and vegetation, Lord of the Sun, who causes the crops to grow, and land and sea to be bathed in light and fertility. Bless and protect me.

- Turn next to the west, the direction of the willing sacrifice, the Corn God who was cut down with the last harvest, sometimes recalled in the Corn Mother created from this sheaf. Touch your right shoulder with your right hand and say:

Blessed are you who offered your body as the corn that there might be new life once more after a necessary period of fallow. Bless and protect me.

- Turn to the north, the direction of the Earth Mother who brings forth the new Sun/Corn God on the midwinter solstice. Touch your left shoulder with your right hand and say:

Blessed are you, womb of the earth who gives and takes life, only to renew it. Bless and protect me.

- Finally turn to each of the four directions, clasping both hands over your heart saying:

Protected and blessed in love, so may it be.

The Kabbalistic (Qabalistic) cross

The traditional version of this ritual uses the names of the spheres of light, or splendid sapphires on the Kabbalistic Tree of Life, that form a mystical representation of the bi-directional link between the individual person and the godhead. The Tree of Life, with its ten spheres and 22 interconnecting pathways, is at the heart of Jewish mystical tradition, but even if you do not understand the deeper philosophy it can form an important and powerful symbol for spiritual work and especially for protection. As you use the ritual, visualise rays of light and coloured jewels radiating all round you, as though you were standing beneath this great, mystical tree, looking upwards. The nearest I have come to understanding it was when I performed this ritual at night beneath a huge tree, looking up through the branches at the moon and stars overhead.

This tends to be more solemn than the Wiccan Cross ritual (see page 144), and can be used when you feel afraid or especially vulnerable. Perform it very slowly, enunciating each word and visualising the cross of light forming within you as you touch the different parts of your body. The movements are almost identical to those in the Wiccan Cross, but this time instead of celebrating, for example, the goddess as manifest in her different aspects through the changing seasons, the words focus on a single source of divinity or light, radiating all round you. You can visualise your own personal source of goodness – the first sphere, at the top of the Tree of Light, called *Kether*, or the Crown, is described as an emanation of pure white light from the undifferentiated life force that has no beginning and no end. This time you do not form a circle.

- Stand straight as before and touch your forehead with your right hand in the centre of your brow, saying:

  So art thou, so am I connected to divine light
  and protection within myself.

- Bring your hand down in a straight line, visualising this as a shaft of light, to touch your genitals or womb, saying:

  So art thou the Kingdom on Earth, so am I connected
  and rooted within my body.

- Touch your right shoulder and say:

  So art thou the Power, so am I protected from all harm
  by thy Divine Power.

- Draw a line across your body with your right hand, to touch your left shoulder, and say:

  So art thou the Glory, so am I illumined by thy glory.

- Clasp your hands in front of your body, over your heart and say:

  For ever and ever.

- Finally, extend your hands and arms to form a cross as you say either: *Aum* (the sound that according to Buddhists and Hindus brought the universe into being), or *Amen*.

Flower essences

Over recent years flower essences have become increasingly recognised as a potent form of healing. Because they are made by leaving flowers in sunlight – thus absorbing the essence of light and the flower rather than having pharmaceutical properties – they are gentle and safe for use with adults, children, animals and plants. Unlike flower or herb preparations they have no odour. They also have no medical properties but act on the soul or spirit and because they are filled with light are especially potent for combating negativity. Flower essences are especially good because negativity that is removed is replaced by a corresponding strength.

You can absorb the protection or offer it to a loved one by placing a few drops of the dilute essence on the tongue, in a dropper or in a glass of water to be sipped perhaps during the evening to induce calm and sleep or in the morning to steady them for the day ahead. Over a period of time you may find that the anti-bullying drink does make your child more able to cope or prepares your partner to outface a critical boss.

Flower essences also provide a way of strengthening a person's vulnerable mind, so that they can make wise decisions for themselves. The essences do this without interfering with the free will, for they do not work against people's will, but instead introduce positive light. This is particularly useful where someone is unable to recognise or acknowledge potential hazards. For example, teenagers may be overly influenced by someone who offers excitement, without realising that they may also represent danger; or they may be dazzled by an affluent but superficial older person who offers instant gratification.

Choosing flower essences

The flower essences, especially the Bach remedies, are widely available in pharmacies as well as alternative health stores. To help you make your choice, look in Further Reading (see page 179) and Useful Contacts (see page 182). You will also find information in promotional material at pharmacies. If in doubt, hold a crystal pendulum over a list of essences and ask your pendulum to indicate with a positive swing the most appropriate essence to help you. If more than one is selected, you can use a drop of each. However, do not worry too much about choosing the right one: if you do choose one that is not right, it will have no effect at all.

I have concentrated primarily on the Bach Flower Remedies, since these are available worldwide and are especially helpful for protective work. Dr Edward Bach (1886–1936) was a British medical consultant, homeopath and bacteriologist who believed that daily life could create negative reactions in a person that would eventually cause illness and disease. The natural vibrations of his flower remedies restore the balance by triggering the body's defence system to restore mental harmony and thereby the health of the whole person.

I have grouped the Bach remedies according to their different purposes and listed one or two that I find particularly helpful for psychic protection work. I have then also suggested essences from other creators round the world, such as Desert Alchemy, Alaskan Flower and Harebell Flower Essences, that have powerful protective functions.

Bach Flower Essence Remedies for fright

Aspen

Negative response: Irrational, free-floating fears, apprehension of the malevolence of an unknown power or disaster of unknown origin; fear of sleeping, rooted in vivid troubling dreams.

Symptoms: Sleep disturbances, especially sleep-walking and talking in sleep, headaches, anxiety and subsequent exhaustion because of inability to rest, sudden attacks of faintness.

Positive outcome: Trusting the unknown future, with a sense of being protected and a feeling of security.

Cherry plum

Negative response: Feelings of losing control and of acting out negative emotions.

Symptoms: Obsessive fears, delusions, suicidal fears or nervous breakdown.

Positive outcome: Calmness, emotional and mental stability, inner security to confront fears.

Mimulus

Negative response: Recognised but often secret fears of specific situations, for example of dogs, heights or enclosed spaces; fear of mortality and loneliness or of illness and pain.

Symptoms: Intolerance of noise, crowds or situations where there may be conflict; rapid, shallow breathing, blushing or stuttering.

Positive outcome: Courage to face up to fears, but also recognition of the value of one's own sensitivity and sense of privacy.

Red chestnut
Negative response: Fear and anxiety over the welfare of others, anticipating problems that may never occur.

Symptoms: Over-concern for global issues, projecting personal worries on to others, rather than acknowledging them.

Positive outcome: Allowing others to cope with their own problems, with confidence that they will manage.

Rock rose
Negative response: Feelings of alarm and panic, being paralysed by fear.

Symptoms: Trembling, feeling intensely cold and experiencing nightmares.

Positive outcome: Courage to face a sudden crisis, a calm response to problems.

Bach Flower Essence Remedies for uncertainty

Agrimony
Negative response: Anxieties hidden from the world by cheerfulness, hiding inner turmoil without complaint.

Symptoms: May use alcohol, drugs and other stimulants or tranquillisers to relieve inner mental pain, be restless, take risks and seek excitement.

Positive outcome: Acknowledging own feelings and fears and so moving to a real sense of peace.

Centaury
Negative response: Undifferentiated conformity to ideas of others, too eager to please, so easily exploited and dominated.

Symptoms: Shoulders and back may be stiff or painful, reflecting the need to fit into a mould created by others.

Positive outcome: Ability to act decisively, trust own judgement and draw boundaries.

Cerato
Negative response: Lack of confidence in own abilities, lacking trust in own judgement and intuition.

Symptoms: Relying too much on the advice of others; being easily misled and changing mind frequently; over-sensitivity to ideas and influences.

Positive outcome: Confidence to rely on own judgement and develop individuality.

Holly

Negative response: Overwhelmed by negative emotions, jealousy, envy, anger, suspicion and the urge for revenge.

Symptoms: Unable to respond positively without bitterness or aggressiveness breaking out.

Positive outcome: Promotes feelings of goodwill in oneself and so towards others, awareness that the answer is in spreading positivity which will be evident in a personal sense of well-being.

Walnut

Negative response: Offers protection from external influences that impinge on progress of free choice and security at times of major life changes, for example adolescence, career, marriage, the birth of a child.

Symptoms: Uncertainty, fear of leaving old patterns of life, feeling shaken to the core as old certainties fade.

Positive outcome: Breaking the link with redundant ways of operating, discovering own new identity.

Desert Alchemy Essences

Canyon grapevine: Good for finding a balance between alienation and a sense of entrapment; clarifies dominance and dependency issues, and helps to turn obstacles into opportunities.

Cardon: Good for releasing personal negativity, especially where repressed or denied, so that the shadow side becomes a source of strength and confidence.

Coral bean: Activates survival instincts in face of present or past danger.

Sow thistle: Counteracts negative and destructive behaviour whether in self or others, gives power to resist intimidation and overpowering personalities of others.

Alaskan Flower Essences

Grass of Parnassus (Parnassia palustris): Introduces the cleansing and nourishing benefits of light energies; helps one to release fully the energy of past experiences so that they can be brought to completion on all levels.

Monkshood (Aconitum delphinifolium): Offers protection and support when encountering and integrating one's shadow self; also helps to connect with one's own divinity, leading to more positive interactions with others.

Harebell Flower Essences

Cymbidium: Useful for resisting those who undermine confidence.

Elder: For protection in potentially abusive situations; good for confronting and overcoming a sense of helplessness.

Marjoram: Protects against harm and strengthens nerve in times of danger.

Speedwell: Offers safe travel and calm in crisis situations.

Thistle: Maintains integrity in difficult situations.

Tormentil: Helps in resisting people who would crush and overwhelm and increases self-esteem.

Using flower essences

Experiment until you find those that seem to work well for you. Different family members may find certain essences particularly protective – my own personal favourite all-purpose protective essence remains the Glastonbury Thorn Essence. Legend says that when Joseph of Arimathea brought the Holy Grail to England in AD 64, he rested his staff on the ground and from this sprang the tree which is the source of the essence. Whether or not the legend is true, the essence has a reputation for bringing courage and staying power, as well as repelling negative, unwise and hostile influences.

To use the essence, scatter a few drops of essence diluted in pure spring water around the sufferer's bed or add a few drops of floral radiance to their bath water – you can offer to run it.

You can also sprinkle a calming flower essence that promotes calm and peaceful sleep on the pillows of small children, to prevent nightmares or insomnia. Adults who have disturbed sleep may also find this beneficial.

School or work bags or coats can be circled with a few drops of essence diluted in spring water. If you need to be unobtrusive, use a room spray with pure spring water before the family comes down to breakfast.

Flower essences are also good for offering protection and healing to streams, the sea and wasteland. On the dawn of the third millennium, my young son Bill and I made our protective offerings to sea and stream where I live on the Isle of Wight.

- Whenever you use your essences, by sprinkling them or adding them to a bath, try to create pools of light with which to amplify them. Best of all, of course, is sunlight or moonlight, but you can also use candlelight, electric light or fibre optic light – if children are around, you can blow out candles once you have created the light pool.

- When you add the essence or sprinkle the essence water, say:

  Light within, light above, keep safe flower heart, those I love.

To make a dilute mixture

The usual dosage is two to four drops, or a single drop for a young child or animal. **If you are pregnant, seek medical advice before using flower essences.**

As with homeopathy, diluted formulae work as well as or better than more concentrated ones, so that a weaker, more frequent, dosage is more effective than a stronger one.

- Place two drops from each chosen stock remedy into a small bottle of water (about 30 ml/2 tbsp), adding a little brandy as a preservative if desired. If you do not wish to use alcohol, use apple cider vinegar or honey. Honey is excellent for using for children and pets, who should be given a very dilute mix of the essences.

- Read the label of each essence carefully as they can vary from type to type, and if in doubt ask the pharmacist where you purchase them for detailed instructions.

- Before use, gentle shake the remedy bottle to awaken the living energies.

Although it may take months to change a deep-seated trauma, you may find that you or your loved one begins to feel more positive quite soon after beginning to use a flower essence. With an ongoing situation, such as long-term educational, work or relationship difficulties or a chronic condition, you may find it helpful to change after a few weeks to another essence with very similar properties.

NINE

Chakra and Aura Protection

An aura is the personal psychic energy field made up of different colours and levels, surrounding the whole body, but usually perceived most clearly around the head; it is seen by the clairvoyant or psychic inner eye, and some people can see it physically.

All people and living things, and even inanimate objects, are said to possess an aura. Animate life creates a stronger and thereby more visible aura, because of the interactive energy flowing between it and the auras of other people and the environment. Tradition says that auric energy is created by the *chakras*, psychic energy vortexes through which energy flows from the cosmos and Earth into different places in the physical body and mind. Chakra energy is often pictured as a series of brilliant, whirling, multi-coloured lotus petals.

Most traditions locate chakras vertically along the axis of the body, either on or just in front of the backbone; however, they are linked with and take their names from locations on the front of the body, such as the navel, heart, throat and brow.

The universal life force, or *prana,* is said to be filtered via psychic channels, or *nadis,* down the chakra system, each chakra transforming the energy into an appropriate form.

Each of the seven main chakras corresponds to and energises one of the levels of the aura. So each chakra colour radiates its particular vibration, both within the body and as a halo around it. You may find that you can already actually see the aura, whether in your mind's vision or as an external ellipse. Medieval painters depicted the golden aura as haloes around saints and angels.

If an aura seems dull or streaked with dark spots or jagged lines, this would indicate that the subject's body and mind have been subject to negativity that has become trapped in the auric field and so needs psychic first aid. If you hold your hands a few centimetres from your head, you may feel the outline of the aura as a slight resistance to pressure. Trace the line round. If the aura has been subject to stress, it may feel jagged or contain holes.

Practise now seeing the aura around a friend or family member when they are framed against a pale background. If you find this difficult, look just beyond and to the side of the head, and then close your eyes and let colours form in your mind's vision. There are usually one or sometimes two main colours you can see and these can indicate the predominant mood or concern of the person; if a colour is dull or streaked, it indicates an area where there are blockages. Trust your psychic vision and, as your confidence increases with practice, you will before long be able to sense when an aura is blocked, whether or not you can actually see it around the person with your physical eye.

The seven major chakras

The root or base chakra, or maladhara

This is the Earth chakra and its colour is red. It is associated with physical functioning, basic instincts and the five physical senses.

Physical pain and discomfort are manifest at this level and pain and fever may appear as a murky red either in the whole aura or close to an afflicted area of the body or the source of the infection. The root chakra is located at the base of the spine, seat of the *kundalini*, or basic energy source. It is linked with the legs, feet, skeleton and the large intestine.

This chakra creates red, raw energy to overcome fearsome odds and offers courage to make any necessary changes in your life. Blockages can be reflected in problems with legs, feet and bones and in bowel discomfort. On a psychological level, unreasonable anger at trivial causes can often be a symptom.

The sacral chakra, or svadisthana

This is the Moon chakra and its colour is orange. It is associated with spontaneous feelings and urges, and with self-esteem and self-identity.

Though seated in the reproductive system, and so linked with fertility, it focuses on different aspects of comfort or satisfaction, such as eating, drinking and sexuality. It controls the blood, the reproductive system, kidneys, circulation and bladder.

This chakra will put you in touch with your ever-reliable gut feelings and help in matters of fertility in the widest sense. Blockages can be reflected in problems with the reproductive system, bladder and circulation. On a psychological level, irritability and disorders involving physical indulgence can result.

The solar plexus, or manipura

This is the Sun chakra and its colour is yellow. It is associated with the conscious mind, logic, mental power and self-control.

This chakra is seated just below the navel. It controls the digestion, liver, spleen, stomach and small intestine. It is said to absorb the life force, or prana, from living food such as fruit, vegetables and seeds.

This is the energy centre of digesting experiences, taking what is of use from life and casting aside what is redundant, and above all giving us a sense of what is of worth, so creating our sense of integrity and uniqueness.

Blockages in this area may be reflected in ulcers, indigestion, problems with the liver, gall bladder, spleen and stomach, yellowish skin and feelings of nausea. Eating disorders such as anorexia and bulimia also have their seat here when the balance of eating is upset and food necessary for strength and growth becomes attached to an emotional trigger.

On a psychological level, obsessions and over-concern for trivial detail can also result.

The heart chakra, or anahata

This is the chakra of the winds and its colour is green. It is associated with relationships and with emotional stability and harmony within the self as well as with others.

This chakra is situated in the centre of the chest, its energies radiating over the heart, lungs, breasts and the arms and hands, which hold others in love.

The heart chakra is the centre of channelled emotions of altruism, compassion, unconditional love, sympathy and connection with both people and the environment, especially the natural world. Blockages can be reflected in heart palpitations, coughs and colds, lung problems and pains in the hands and arms. On a psychological level, free-floating anxiety or depression can follow an imbalance in this area.

The throat chakra, or vishuddha

This is the chakra of time and space and its colour is blue. It is associated with communication and idealism, the synthesis of emotion and thought.

It is situated close to the Adam's apple in the centre of the neck. As well as the throat and speech organs and thyroid gland, the throat chakra controls the neck and shoulders and the passages that run up to the ears.

The throat chakra is the gateway between a personal and more global perspective and controls ideas, ideals and listening as well as speaking and giving creative and artistic form to thoughts. It is also the seat of the natural sense of justice and the transformation of experience into conscious wisdom.

If things are wrong in these areas, you may suffer sore throats, colds, swollen glands and thyroid problems. Blockages can also be reflected in problems with the neck, shoulders, speech organs, mouth, jaws and teeth and throat. On a psychological level, confusion and incoherence result from an imbalance here.

The third eye or brow chakra, or savikalpa samadhi

This is the chakra of freedom and its colour is purple or indigo. It is associated with unconscious wisdom and psychic powers, especially clairvoyance, but also clairaudience and mediumistic abilities.

It is situated just above the bridge of the nose, in the centre of the brow, and controls the eyes, ears and both hemispheres of the brain.

The brow chakra is the centre of inspiration and an awareness of a world beyond the material and immediate. At this level, you may communicate with your Higher Self and angelic/spirit guides and be able to see into past worlds. With the opening of this chakra, your healing powers take on a truly spiritual dimension, especially for absent healing, drawing on higher power. In your everyday life, the power of this chakra is manifest as a highly sensitised intuitive awareness.

When this chakra is not functioning properly, you may experience frequent headaches, earache, noises in your ears, eye infections or temporary blurring of vision that has no organic cause. On a psychological level, insomnia or nightmares can result.

The crown chakra, or nirvakelpa samadhi

This is the chakra of eternity and its colour is violet, merging with white light. This white, the source of pure light, is made up of all the other colours combined, and in this form it pours upwards and outwards into the cosmos, and downwards and inwards from the cosmos back into the crown.

The crown chakra is situated at the top of the head in the centre and rules the brain, body and psyche, growth and well-being – physical, mental and spiritual. It is the centre of evolved creative and spiritual energy and represents pure spiritual awareness and connection with higher planes; it is the state in which mystical experiences occur.

Blockages can be reflected in problems with the sinuses, skin and scalp and in general viruses and infections in the whole body that do not easily clear. You may feel tired but unable to relax, worried but unable to focus your actions on solutions. You may suffer a series of minor accidents and have a permanent cold. On a psychological level, an inability to rise above everyday and material concerns, alienation from friends and family and a rigid attitude can result.

Cleansing and protecting the chakras

You may experience tension or pain when a blockage occurs; or you may see or sense the problems in the aura; or you may feel absolutely fine. But whatever the case, regular chakra cleansing is like brushing your teeth before bed, a necessary regular exercise. You should cleanse your chakras at least once a month; in addition, you should cleanse them whenever you feel exhausted or enervated or in times of high activity or stress in your life. This simple process is probably the most routine and effective form of psychic protection and ensures your psychic, physical and emotional systems are sufficiently clear to be restored in sleep and naturally energised to maximise the positive aspects of your daily world.

Each chakra has an associated fragrance that can be evoked either in incense or as an oil. The Native North Americans used the process of 'smudging', wafting the smoke from sweet grass, cedar and sage over themselves for cleansing and also for empowerment of mind, body and soul. You can create similar energies by burning incense or oil in specific fragrances that purify the different chakras if they are blocked or filled with stagnant energies.

If you are pregnant or suffering from any chronic medical condition, you must consult your doctor before using any oils or essences.

By burning a chakra fragrance chosen from the list below, you can increase the energies flowing from that particular chakra to your aura and this can help to remove any anxieties or doubts in your general life. For example, if you feel confused and over-emotional, you should burn a cleansing solar plexus fragrance, for example lemon, pine or sage; this will have the effect of stimulating the faculties of that chakra and its associated level in the aura, to clear your mind and bring logic and determination to the situation. Similarly, if you are facing a confrontation or are being attacked, you should burn ginger or cinnamon to activate your root survival energy. Lavender is an all-purpose chakra cleanser.

Look at the list below for full details of the fragrances and the areas for which they are appropriate. If in doubt as to which energy you need, place a variety of incenses or bottles of oil relating to the different chakras and hold a pendulum over each in turn. It will circle clockwise or pull down as if suddenly heavy over the appropriate one – you may be surprised at the source of the blockage it indicates, but the pendulum is remarkably accurate.

Incenses and the chakra

Crown chakra: Bergamot, frankincense, sandalwood

Brow chakra: Geranium, myrrh, violet

Throat chakra: Eucalyptus, lemongrass, peppermint

Heart chakra: Chamomile, lavender, rose

Solar plexus chakra: Lemon, pine, sage

Sacral chakra: Orange, jasmine, ylang-ylang

Root chakra: Basil, patchouli, tea-tree

A ritual to cleanse the whole system of negativity

If you have been drained of energy by an argument or a difficult work situation, you could send energy and light throughout your entire system and aura by surrounding yourself with one of each of the chakra incenses. This method, which works best with incense sticks, is also good for relieving personal fears that can so easily throw us off balance.

- Stand your incense sticks in deep upright containers (old bottles are ideal) at a safe distance from yourself and any fabrics or flammable substances.

- Make a comfortable place to lie down by placing cushions on the floor. (You can lie on the sofa or on your bed if you prefer.)

- Place a jar or bottle containing a crown chakra incense stick such as frankincense to the north of where you intend to lie down. You can either use a compass to find north, or estimate it from a known location near your home.

- Position your body where you intend to lie down.

- At brow level, on either side of your head, stand the brow-chakra incense; then place the appropriate chakra incenses on both sides of your body level with your throat, heart, navel and womb or genitals. Finally, place a single root chakra incense to the south of your feet.

- Light the sticks in the order of placing and lie down, visualising the smoke as the different chakra colours, swirling in bands, both within and beyond your body in the auric field around you, forming a rainbow of light and healing.

- Visualise energies spiralling upwards and downwards, converging and filling you with radiant colour. You may see your whole body as a rainbow.

- Wait until the incense is burned through and use the time to weave dreams and allow images and sounds to form that may speak of events to come or possible pathways you might follow.

Cleansing the chakras with a pendulum

You can also unblock specific chakras by revolving a crystal pendulum over them nine times in an anti-clockwise direction. When this is done, turn the pendulum clockwise to infuse the chakra with light. If you can work in sunlight with the sunbeams casting rainbows in your pendulum, that is especially potent.

A ritual to cleanse the whole mind and body

This is another way of spring-cleaning your chakra system which can be done at monthly intervals.

- Hold your pendulum over the crown chakra, allowing it to turn anti-clockwise nine times. Repeat this with each of the seven chakras, ending with the root chakra in the small of your back.

- Finally, revolve your pendulum over first your left and then your right foot, nine times. Do not energise the chakras as you unblock them, as the weight of negative energies will weaken the potency of the pendulum.

- When you have removed negative energy from your feet (also associated with the root chakra), shake your pendulum over the ground, preferably over soil or grass in the open air, to allow Earth energies to transform the negativity into new growth.

- Next, plunge your pendulum into cold water nine times and shake it dry. You have now purified your pendulum with the elements of Earth and Water.

- Now, beginning with the right foot, reverse the order you used in cleansing, this time revolving your pendulum nine times clockwise over each chakra, ending at the crown.

- Pass it nine times either through a pool of sunlight or a golden candle flame to re-energise with Fire and Air.

Closing the chakras

Your chakras are gatekeepers to your body and mind and so through them filter all kinds of impressions, psychic and earthly, positive and negative. So even if you have been carrying out entirely positive psychic or divinatory work and had an exciting rather than a stressful day, your mind can be racing and you may be unable to relax and settle to sleep. This exercise can help at such a time to close your body, mind and soul to external impressions, like locking the front and back doors of your home at night after a party when the last revellers have gone home. It is also excellent if you feel suddenly vulnerable, if you are either in the presence of a hostile or intrusive person or in an environment in which you are aware you need to protect yourself by shutting out negative impressions.

You can do this either by visualisation or, if you have more time and the opportunity, by using crystals, as explained below. If you are using crystals, place each stone from the circle of crystals you make in a bag or box after using it on the appropriate chakra, so that gradually your circle is removed.

As you work, imagine each revolving centre of energy within you slowing, the light fading and stillness falling over the area controlled by each chakra.

- Create a circle of seven crystals, using the list of protective crystals in the chapter on Protective Crystals and Metals (see page 87) as a guide.

- Begin with a black stone, for example obsidian, in the north of the circle. Next to it, place a soft purple crystal such as amethyst, then a pale blue crystal, perhaps a blue lace agate, followed by a soft green crystal such as jade, then a soft yellow crystal, such as calcite, then a gentle pink crystal, perhaps rose quartz, and finally a muted brown, such as a pebble you have found on the shore, or brown jasper.

- Take first the black stone from the circle and place it on the crown of your head, gently closing your crown chakra. As you do so, see pure white energy filtering downwards to your third eye chakra in the centre of your brow, transforming into soft purple.

- Place your purple crystal from the circle on your third eye chakra and gently close the chakra, visualising the purple moving downwards to your throat chakra, and merging into a soft misty blue.

- Next, place the pale blue crystal on your throat chakra. See your chakra gently closing and the blue light moving down to the region of your heart, becoming turquoise as it merges with the green of this chakra.

- Use your green crystal to slow down and close the heart chakra, so that the green moves downwards to merge with the yellow of your solar plexus chakra, just below the navel.

- Use your yellow crystal to slow down this chakra, with the yellow becoming orange and moving down to the sacral chakra close to your reproductive system.

- Hold your pink crystal over your womb or genitals to close this chakra and the light will become a pale, transparent red and return to the root chakra at the base of your spine.

- Use a brown crystal, for example jasper, to mute the natural red energies, so that they will sleep at the base of your spine until you need their power again. This root energy, called kundalini, is frequently pictured as a coiled snake.

If you are not using crystals, you can visualise the chakras one by one, beginning with the crown; imagine the whirling petals moving more slowly as their contact with other dimensions and the outer world is closed down.

Though I recommend lying or sitting on cushions or a bed, you can carry out this visualisation absolutely anywhere or at any time when you feel anxieties rising. As I hate travelling in enclosed lifts, this is an exercise I carry out so that I do not panic – sometimes we need to protect ourselves from inner as well as outer fears.

Chakras and auras

Auras and chakras are inextricably entwined and cleansing chakras will automatically have a positive effect on the aura. This connection is bi-directional and so by working directly on the aura you will also automatically unblock and energise your chakra system.

Your aura is the reception area for all kinds of inputs and energies, positive and negative, from the external world, that are unconsciously as well as consciously projected, and so it becomes tangled and full of other people's angers and worries. Like tangled, dirty hair, it needs to be washed and conditioned to remove the impurities accumulated through everyday living.

Even the constant chattering of children or a friend or colleague when you are trying to work can tangle your aura of harmony. Your aura can also be adversely affected by pollution, stress, overwork, junk food and lack of fresh air. You can remove these ill-effects before they reach your physical body by cleansing the aura, thus giving energy and harmony to your body and mind to replace any negativity.

Cleansing the aura

It is a good idea to cleanse your aura once a week, and every fourth week combine it with the chakra fragrance cleansing (see page 158). Though some people prefer to cleanse the aura in the morning, bedtime is a good time to remove the day's negativity, so that you will enjoy restful sleep and wake naturally energised.

Cleansing by colour breathing

Cleansing and balancing by colour breathing are good ways of beginning a day or relaxing after stress, but you can also use the technique in a modified form, whenever it is needed. You may want to use it while waiting in a supermarket queue or on a railway station, in which case you can stand or walk to make your breathing less obvious; the important thing is to visualise the colours.

For all-over auric cleansing, you can visualise yourself inhaling white or golden light and exhaling dark or black light.

- Look in the mirror and see what are the predominant colours of your aura (there may be more than one) – or close your eyes and picture it. If you cannot get in touch with auric colours, draw or paint a variety of different hues of all the main rainbow colours, plus pink, black, silver, gold, turquoise, grey and brown. Make them harsh and clear, gentle and murky.

- Hold your pendulum over each of the hues in turn, asking first which is predominant, then if any are missing. Your pendulum will as before respond either with a clockwise swing or by pulling down.

As an alternative method, try working from the chakra colours listed on pages 154–7 that will be reflected in your aura. You should be able to estimate the colours that are present in excess by your feelings and/or your current situation. So, for example, if you have had an argument or suffered an injustice, your aura may be flooded with a harsh red. However, if someone has been trying to blackmail you emotionally, a dull green aura may be present. You can then use the antidote colours listed below to restore the balance. If you feel depressed, you can be fairly certain your aura will be dark grey or even black. If the hue seems murky or harsh your system is suffering from an excess of negativity, or hostility from others.

If a colour is very pale, then you may be drained of enthusiasm and energy by too many demands and need to concentrate on energising your aura.

For psychic protection and uplifting the spirit, the following combinations seem to work well.

For instant energy or courage in times of danger: Inhale red and exhale blue.

To banish anger: Inhale blue and exhale red.

For confidence when you are being criticised or undermined: Inhale orange and exhale indigo.

To still the mind and spirit after stress: Inhale indigo and exhale orange.

To overcome emotional blackmail: Inhale turquoise and exhale dull green.

To repel jealousy and fears: Inhale violet and exhale yellow.

For the power to repel malevolence: Inhale yellow and exhale violet.

For positivity in any sphere and for banishing depression and despair: Inhale white or gold and exhale black.

To overcome sadness: Inhale pink and exhale grey.

To restore lost colours or colours that have faded: Exhale the paler shade and inhale a brighter one.

To heal any negativity in the aura: Silver can be used, especially if you feel surrounded by a dark cloud and fear psychic attack.

Colour breathing can be used in the morning or at any other time when you need energising or calming. You visualise your breath as different colours, with the negativity appearing as dark, dull or murky hues. You can expel these negative influences from your body as you breathe out, and then balance your aura by introducing lighter, brighter hues.

- Sit comfortably with your feet touching the floor.

- Take a deep breath through your nose and as you do so, tense your body by placing your hands behind your head, with your elbows pointing forward, then move your elbows out so they are parallel with the sides of your head and lean your head back gently.

- Breathe out slowly though your mouth, releasing your arms and extending them as widely as possible at shoulder height, stretching like a cat awaking from a sleep.

- Return them to your lap or sides, whichever feels most comfortable.
- Breathe in slowly; hold this breath for a slow count of three (one…and… two…and…three), then exhale slowly through your mouth with a sigh.
- Do this five or six times.
- Visualise the air you are inhaling as pure white or golden light, radiating through your body.
- Exhale slowly, seeing black mist being expelled, leaving your body lighter and more harmonious.
- Slow your breathing a little more, letting the golden or white light enter your lungs and spread throughout your body.
- Repeat the pattern, each time visualising the dark mist leaving your body becoming paler as the negativity is expelled, until your outward breath is quite clear. Your aura is now cleansed.

You can also adapt this method for specific colour breathing, using the combinations given on page 163.

Use your exhaled breath as before to banish negativity and your inhaled colour to introduce calm or energy, according to your needs. The warmer colours – red, yellow and orange – are stimulating and energising for the aura; the cooler colours – blue, green and purple – soothe and gently uplift.

Experiment with different colour combinations and monitor mood changes.

When you feel totally balanced and harmonious and ready for either action or sleep – depending on which colours you breathed – stretch once more and, as you circle your hands around your head and shoulders, feel the renewed colours either moving slowly and in harmony or whirling with energy and optimism.

TEN

Travel and Workplace Protection

Travel protection

The earliest amulets and rituals were created to protect the hunter, and some of these survive today in societies that still follow the nomadic way of life. Travelling today, whether over long distances or commuting to work, can be hazardous, as predatory wild beasts and brigands have been replaced by high-speed vehicles, road rage and supersonic aircraft flying daily through overcrowded skies. Psychic travel insurance is as important today as it was when our ancestors crossed the oceans in their long boats or followed the herds over difficult and dangerous terrain.

According to tradition, in the Kei Islands to the south-west of New Guinea, as soon as a ship set sail for a far-off port, the part of the beach from which it was launched was covered with palm leaves and marked as a sacred place. None might walk on it until the boat returned safely, and the leaves would be renewed if any blew away or withered. To protect the voyagers, three pure maidens remained in a room absolutely motionless while the ship was actually at sea, crouched on mats with their hands around their knees. They were not allowed to turn their heads or make any sudden movements or, it was believed, the ship would toss on the ocean. Nor were they permitted to eat any sticky substances that might slow the passage of the ship through the waves. Once it was estimated that the ship had reached land safely, the girls were able to move more freely. However, for the whole time the travellers were away, the girls were not allowed to eat fish with sharp bones and stings in case the absent voyagers injured themselves. Thankfully, the rituals we use today are not so arduous.

A *modern ritual for a happy and safe journey*

This is a ritual I have used many times. I have modified it only slightly from earlier versions I learned.

- Pack and prepare early for your business trip or holiday, allowing plenty of time to catch any connections. This ensures that you start in a calm frame of mind (if travelling companions insist on last-minute panics, let them fret alone).

- When all is ready, go to a quiet place, a garden or a well-loved room. Into a bowl of clear water, gently drop a dark protective crystal, such as jet, smoky quartz, a garnet or bloodstone, a moonstone if you will be travelling at night or a shell if voyaging by sea or to a destination near a river or lake or by the seaside.

- As the ripples spread outwards, light a blue candle for travel and protection, saying:

    Candle fire, candlelight, guard and guide me, day and night.

- Drop a little wax into the water, so that it hisses and sets on the surface, forming land (the Earth element) to represent your safe arrival on terra firma. You may find the wax makes a shape reminiscent of the country you will be visiting or of your mode of transport.

- Blow out the candle and let the smoke travel upwards, carrying you above any minor setbacks and irritations to the pleasure of at last fulfilling your dreams, saying:

    Candle guardian, candlelight, keep me safe within your sight.

- Visualise the light taking the form of an angel or a being of light, flying before you and enfolding you in a circle of light, shedding doubts and anxiety, ahead of your actual journey.

- Take your protective crystal from the water, dry it and place it in a small leather or fabric bag, with a sprinkling of basil, caraway and rosemary; keep this in your hand luggage.

If your lover or partner is going away, prepare the amulet for him or her, as these herbs are also good for ensuring fidelity during absence.

As you travel, if you feel afraid, say your rhymes silently and invoke the presence of your candle being.

A *crystal ritual for daily journeys*

- Set a circle of protective incense sticks or cones, such as sandalwood or lavender, around a bowl of water.

- Cast the crystal into the bowl of water. As you do so, visualise a perfect journey to work: clear roads, a seat on the train and no delays.

- Light a candle, placing it in a wide candle holder, so that the wax will form a circle around the base.

- As you drip candle wax in the water, drop spots of wax in a circular formation around the crystal, saying:

    Ring of love, ring of calm, day by day keep me from harm.

- Visualise your candle guardian as you blow out the light.

- Dry the crystal and carry it with you in a small bag.

- Let the candle burn through and, with a sharp knife, cut a perfect circle from the wax and on it engrave a protective symbol (see page 59).

- Wrap it in white silk and each evening, or before a significant journey, place it in the bag or case you take to work each day. Before you leave home in the morning, remove it and place it near the door, so that it is one of the first things you see on your return.

Recharge your crystal regularly (see page 89) and replace the wax amulet at regular intervals.

Travelling amulets

One of the most common forms of protection, for churchgoers and non-churchgoers alike, is to carry a talisman or medallion dedicated to one of the saints who guard travellers.

St Christopher, patron saint of travellers
Most famous of all talismans for travel is the St Christopher medallion that is carried or worn by travellers, especially motorists and seafarers, in many parts of the world. The legends surrounding St Christopher, whose name means 'Christ-bearer', have endowed his medallion with magical as well as strictly religious symbolism.

St Christopher was martyred during the persecutions of Decius, at Lycia in Asia Minor in the third century. According to legend, Christopher was a giant-like man who vowed to serve only the most powerful master.

Converted to Christianity, he met a hermit who told him to live a solitary life next to a deep ford and carry travellers across the fast-flowing river on his back. One day a child asked Christopher to carry him across the river. The child appeared to be very small, but to Christopher's surprise, he became heavier and heavier until halfway across Christopher feared they might both be drowned. He asked the child why he was so heavy. The child revealed that he was Christ, struggling beneath the weight of the sins of the world. Immediately the burden was lightened. Christ told Christopher to plant his staff as they reached land, saying that the next day it would bear flowers and golden leaves as a token of God's forgiveness to the world.

Before he died, St Christopher asked God to protect any place where his image was displayed from pestilence, plague and other dangers. In addition, he asked that anyone who looked upon his image should be saved from dying that day. For this reason, pictures of St Christopher are hung in public places and icons and Christopher carvings are erected near gateways and entrances to towns and churches.

St Christopher's image on a medallion is carried today by thousands of travellers to protect them on journeys and many people have held the image in moments of peril.

In 1969, his feast day (25 July) was reduced by the Catholic Church to the status of a local cult because his influence had moved far beyond the Church to secular life. But 25 July is still said to be a particularly fortunate day on which to travel or begin a journey.

Julian the Hospitaller
St Julian is the patron saint of ferrymen, innkeepers, long-distance and impoverished travellers, wandering musicians and circus people.

In penance for killing his parents by mistake, Julian built a hospice for the poor near a wide river and would ferry travellers across the water without charge. One night he took in a leper who was close to death and gave him his own bed. As the man died, Julian saw a vision of the departing soul who assured him that God had forgiven him. Julian's feast day, 12 February, is said to be another lucky day to travel or stay away from home. Although his medallions and images are less common, he is a much-loved protector saint in the Netherlands, and you may find his talisman of use if you are undertaking a lengthy or budget-priced journey.

A ritual to protect your vehicle and passengers
This ritual is useful for protecting your car, bicycle or any other form of transport – and yourself and any passengers. As well as using normal

security devices, you can imprint a vehicle so that it is psychically guarded and therefore less susceptible to theft, vandalism or accident.

- In the early morning, before anyone is around, prepare a strong mint infusion, using freshly gathered mint on which dew or early morning rain has fallen. If you live in an apartment you can use pots of mint. Dried mint will also work well.

- Tear rather than chop the mint and drop it into hot water – you do not need very much infusion – saying as you place the herbs in the water:

    Guardians of the Earth, I ask that you protect my vehicle
    by the power of this herb, to guard and guide.

- Stir in circles from the centre outwards with a wooden spoon or a stick from a protective tree, such as a thorn tree, rowan or willow, repeating:

    Out and away, forever to stay.

- When the infusion has been standing for a few minutes, drain off the herbs, saying:

    Cast away harm, cast away danger,
    Whether from spite or careless stranger.

- Now add to the infusion a pinch of sea salt, saying:

    From perils of nature, from flood and from fire,
    From road rage, misjudgement and other's desire.

- Finally, create a triple circle of protection, beginning close to the vehicle, by sprinkling the infusion clockwise in three circles, beginning with the innermost one, saying:

    Guardians of the Earth, enclose in your threefold protection, from the
    triple dangers accident, nature and evil, and let this vehicle bring joy to
    others as well as myself.

- Tip the remaining infusion into the earth. Later, bury the herbs as near as possible to the place the car or bicycle is kept.

Whatever the mode of transport, it is important that you use it to give pleasure to others – even on a bicycle you can run errands or visit lonely or sick people. Though this may sound very twee and sentimental (even to me as I write it in my late afternoon of plummeting blood sugar grumpiness), the greatest form of protection really is in doing good to others, for if your vehicle becomes associated with happy thoughts then it does automatically attract positive energies.

Protection when flying

Many people fear flying to some degree, and a number are seized by blind panic as the plane leaves the tarmac. Some say that these fears result from buried memories of a disaster in a previous life (a number of people have been regressed to scenes as Second World War pilots, and have recalled military numbers or aircraft details that were later verified independently). Others say that humans are not meant to fly and so panic is a natural, albeit primitive, instinctive reaction to danger.

My own fear of flying was cured rather dramatically after I was caught in the Los Angeles earthquake in 1994 and somehow felt I had used up my hazard quotient, but several people I know have found the following ritual helpful. This is psychic protection at its most positive, enabling us to overcome fears and phobias that may seem to have no logical basis, but can be socially crippling. You can adapt this ritual for different fears.

- Cut nine hairs from your head (the more traditional method involves pulling them out, but I am a coward about such matters).

- Weave them into a hair circle, as you do so binding your terror of flying.

- Plait into the circle dried straws or grasses, saying as you do so:

> Wind and bind, knot and tie,
> Fears and terrors in here lie;
> Twist and turn, tangle, twist,
> Strangling dreads henceforth desist.

- Place your plait in a small, dark-coloured box and tie it firmly with three knots, having twisted threads of dark brown or black so that they are twisted and tangled around the box. Say:

> Three times the sorrow I secure, terrors will no more endure.

- Go into a garden or park on a night when the moon is waning and dig a deep hole. Place the box in it and cover it with soil.

- Sit for a moment in silence, feeling all the fears fading away.

When you fly, choose a window seat if possible. Close your eyes until you are in the air and on a night flight see yourself rising through the warm night sky to the stars; in the daytime, visualise climbing a rainbow and floating through fields of cascading sunbeams, making the noise and surging movement part of your scenario.

Move among the stars and planets or beams of light; when you hear the announcement that it is safe to remove your seat belt, look out of the window and visualise a guardian either floating on top of the fluffy clouds or dancing above the lights below or on the darkness.

Allow your guardian to assume the most natural form – do not force an identity, just let it come. This may be an angel, a spirit guide, an ancient deity or even a galactic hero or a cartoon character. A friend saw Mickey Mouse on the plane wing and was so surprised she burst out laughing, to the horror of the very serious guy sitting next to her in Business Class. But Mickey cured her fear of flying.

If there is turbulence, return to your sunbeams or stars and close your eyes, allowing the movement to weave itself into your ongoing story. If you do panic, repeat the tying and burying ritual in your mind, reciting the chant silently and seeing yourself sitting quietly as dusk falls.

When the announcement is made that the plane is beginning the descent, ask your guide to transport you to a hot air balloon on which you can descend at your own rate, watching the toy cars and houses below getting larger. When the steep descent begins to the runway, close your eyes once more and slide down a chute in the playground as you did in childhood and land on soft grass.

Repeat the scenario whenever you fly and in time you will find that you are omitting parts and connecting with the actual journey with interest. Alternatively, create scenario of your own for ascending and landing.

Repeat the plaiting ritual before every flight; remember to take a little box and dark thread in your case for the return journey – you can bury it in the sand or float it on the tide if you prefer.

Your guardian may change from flight to flight – allow him or her just to appear without any effort on your part.

Workplace protection

Some workplaces feel naturally welcoming the second you walk through the door. My publisher in Sweden has an office filled with crystals, dreamcatchers, comfortable chairs and lovely music. The fragrance of coffee and fresh flowers pervades the air, the whole place is full of laughter and people seem to flow from one area to the other; efficiency is high and days off for ill-health remarkably few. The managing director shares mealtimes with the workers and will bring in cakes for special occasions. Yet the building is actually a warehouse on an industrial estate.

Contrast this with a similar office I know in London's prestigious Docklands; it has panoramic views and state of the art décor, where interior designers and feng shui experts have vied to create harmony. Yet there is a very high degree of absenteeism, often related to psychosomatic illnesses and minor accidents, and constant friction between workers as well as strict demarcations between workers and management; output is low with the exception of that of a few work-obsessed individuals.

From my experience of both visiting and working in a variety of environments from the factory floor to the television studio I have concluded that where people personalise their working space so that it becomes a part of them (rather than them being a part of it), health and harmony are far more marked and productivity increases dramatically. They feel less threatened by others and so are less territorial. It seems, then, that the open-plan office needs to become a series of mini homes-from-home if it is to function efficiently.

It is as though, by creating a small area, even a locker or corner of the desk with photographs, a few crystals, plants and pictures, a part of one's home is transferred where the individual feels relaxed and receptive to challenges. Add comfortable seating, cushions, flowers, new magazines, juices and fresh coffee on demand and maybe a microwave in a rest area, and productivity really does increase. Scruffy chairs, dingy walls and cracked mugs, plus a machine that produces beverages of indeterminate origin that the workers are expected to pay for, breed negativity as well as germs. On the other hand, where bread, butter and jam, fresh fruit, good-quality towels in the washroom and a quiet room for relaxation are provided by the management, petty thieving and vandalism almost disappear, because people feel that their workplace is an extension of home.

If you do work in a very restrictive environment – and the same applies to impersonal hotels on business trips – try to imprint something of your own personality on the space, so that it becomes part of you. If you work from home, try to keep computers, faxes and work tools in a separate place and to draw a line between collecting the laundry, dealing with family problems and work time and space. Too often those who work from home, even high-earning people, and especially women, are regarded as indulging in a hobby rather than real work. So it is vital for your own positivity to establish limits – you are not a full-time servant and agony aunt who just happens to fit in a high-powered career between feeding the cat, answering the doorbell to itinerant salespersons and evangelists, and ferrying relatives to their various appointments or social events, as is so often expected.

Whether working in and outside the home and especially if you are caring for children, establish a lunch break or at least some time off each day. As a mother of five very untidy children, who works from home, I know as much as anyone the negative, exhausting effects on my serenity of other people's clutter, actual and emotional. I still recall writing a section for a book, entitled *The Aura of Calm*, while two of my family hurled insults at each other across my computer.

All this is central to psychic protection and its ultimate goal, psychic well-being. If you are constantly stressed or feel dehumanised by your working environment, then all the blessing rituals in the world will have no real effect. Clearing away the clutter of your workspace and with it all the bad feelings is the best psychic cleansing of all. If you work from home, a regular ritual bonfire for junk mail, plus some dried rosemary or pine, will fill you with inspiration.

All this good advice is fine and dandy, but if you work with Genghis Khan's big sister or your colleagues are indulging in guerrilla power games with your desk as the refuelling zone, it is hard to avoid feeling invaded.

No employer can apply feng shui to a building and expect instant harmony if there is interpersonal hostility and rivalry over unfair working practices, inequalities of salary or promotion prospects. Nor can you expect to do yourself justice if *Romeo and Juliet* is enacted daily in full view of the office, while you end up doing the work of the lovelorn.

A simple but effective tactic to deflect workplace hassle is to place a large, gentle, protective crystal, such as piece of uncut rose quartz or amethyst with a pointed end, in your personal work space. This can normally be positioned so that it faces a wall, but when an intrusion or hostility comes your way, you can swivel the crystal round to repel the attack. Because the crystal is gentle, it will not harm anyone, but merely act as a barrier, and you may find that your assailant – or the uninvited cabaret act – stops, looks puzzled and goes away.

Alternatively, you can position a small mirror or even your reading glasses so that they reflect towards anyone who approaches at a time when you are busy, or when you think the visitor is bearing problems or burdens to unload. Alexander the Great used this method to good effect in the Valley of the Snakes, reflecting the sunlight in a polished shield. Legend says that the snakes, seeing their own reflections in the mirror, stung themselves to death and Alexander pocketed all the diamonds the serpents had been guarding. You may not get the office gossip-mongers biting themselves to death in the middle of the office in a rabid frenzy but at least they may well take themselves off to another target.

If you are caught in the middle of a difficult phone call and find yourself becoming flustered or angry, circle a rose quartz or amethyst anti-clockwise around the phone as you speak to absorb negativity. Afterwards, plunge your crystal in a bowl of cleansing water that you could keep on your desk. Alternatively, hold the crystal under cold running water in the washroom as soon as possible.

Keep tiny protective crystals or salt in small twists of paper at each corner of your workspace and replace the salt regularly. A small pot of lavender, eau de cologne or roses close by will also help, but rotate plants so they get time to stand in the sun and rest. When you charge your mobile phone, surround it with a circle of dried lavender or rosemary.

If you use e-mail, begin each morning by sending a message to yourself on your office machine: a few lines of a favourite poem, a personal message of empowerment, a soothing image of forests, mountains or your favourite deity of the moment. My youngest son currently uses pictures of Ganesh, the Hindu god of children, on his workbook. Or agree to trade happy e-mails with a friend or colleague. Read them before any other mail and whenever you are feeling under threat and erase them before leaving work.

Finally, if things do get heated and there is an argument at work, extend your hands palm uppermost in front of you as you talk, and with a sweeping gesture push away the negativity. When you feel spite or unfair criticism threatening to engulf you, circle your hands as you reply, still in the palm outwards position, as though you were swimming away.

Afterwards, clear the air when you are alone by turning round three times anti-clockwise, with hands extended in the same position, saying:

> May nought harm me,
> Love calm me,
> Peace alone disarm me.

As soon as possible, take a shower (not a bath), using a pine, mint or tea-tree foam, shaking your fingers to wash off all the anger and bad feelings.

Try to make a reconciliatory or friendly gesture to your opponent the next day, remembering that everything returns threefold to the sender.

A ritual to cleanse negativity from a work area or tools

If there are smoke alarms over your workspace, you can carry out this ritual at home, and visualise your work area. It is especially effective if you take over a job from someone who was unhappy or perhaps was made redundant or if the area feels dark and unfriendly. It is also good for overcoming suspicion towards you if you are a newcomer or have been promoted over colleagues. You can also perform this ritual at home before starting a new job after a period of unemployment or retraining or a period of sickness, to overcome your fears and bad memories of past failures.

- Take two candles – a small black, dark purple or blue one and a large white one.

- Anoint your black or dark-coloured candle with candle dressing oil or a small amount of virgin olive oil for peace, by rubbing the oil into the wax from the top to the bottom with your fingers; as you do so, say,

> *Sorrow, anger, earthwards drain,*
> *Loving things alone remain.*

- Stand your black or dark candle in a dish of sand with a deep, metal bowl of water nearby. As you light it, see all the old redundant energies beginning to melt away.

- Now anoint the white candle, this time working from the bottom to the top, endowing it with all your hopes and plans for the future and saying:

> *Life and hope, skywards wend,*
> *Discord, strife and quarrels, mend.*

- Light the white candle and for a time let the two candles burn down side by side.

- When you are ready, take the dark candle carefully and plunge it into the water, saying:

> *Out, candle, out, cleansed be of what is no longer of worth to me.*

- Leave the white candle to burn down in a safe place.

Dispose of the black candle in an environmentally friendly way; cut a flower shape from the melted white wax and press tiny white quartz crystals or clear glass nuggets into it as an ornament for your workplace.

Negative Earth energies

Negativity in the workplace may also derive from a physical source. In the traditions of both Eastern and Western spirituality can be found the concept that some places may have negative Earth energies and that buildings constructed on them may be affected by these darker vibrations.

Ley lines, the hypothetical lines joining prehistoric sacred sites, are said to be the source of powerful psychic energies, and existing or former mine workings can also sour the energy of buildings erected on top. It is said that people, animals and plants can be adversely affected by locations where tragic events or human sorrow occurred over a period of time; some modern offices are built on the site of former poorhouses, abattoirs, mental hospitals, prisons, workhouses and orphanages where charges were badly treated, and the unhappiness seeps into the soil.

The Chinese talk of adverse or bad energy, or *sha ch'i*, energy that travels in a straight line, accumulating in what they call 'poisoned arrows' that can be created by the sharp corners and diagonals from adjoining buildings or badly positioned furniture. Negative energy or sha ch'i is sometimes called 'tiger energy'.

Some Western researchers attribute negative Earth forces to Hartmann and Curry energy fields. These fields are named after their discoverers and are said to divide the earth into square lattices. Where two Curry lines or Hartmann lines cross, strong energies occur. Where a Curry cross and a Hartmann cross coincide, the effect is doubled.

Other theorists, for example Dr Arthur Bailey, creator of the Bailey Flower Essences and expert on dowsing, attribute problems to black streams, the vast network of underground veins of water that have become polluted psychically – and sometime physically – for reasons I have suggested above.

You can test for any negative energies by walking around your workplace (or indeed your home, for all these factors can affect a house or apartment) with a pendulum. Where your pendulum feels heavy or swings in an anti-clockwise or negative mode, it may be a site of these darker energies.

You may find a wavy line, which would indicate water, or a straight line for a ley line, or even a grid pattern; in the latter case the pendulum may spin round negatively several times.

Neutralising negative Earth energies

If your desk or chair is over the spot, move it or place a dark stone or crystal on a piece of equipment on your desk above the place.

Amethyst crystals are perhaps the most effective stones for neutralising all forms of negative Earth energies. Small amethyst inclusions, still in the rock, are not expensive and make excellent paperweights or ornaments. Rose quartz too will take away any jagged edges of harsh energy. Position these near the centre of the spot of negative energy.

Fresh flowers or a pot plant above the place of negative power will also absorb any bad feelings. African violets and aloe vera are especially effective. You may need to replace these frequently as it is not a conducive spot for growth, so try to rotate hard-working plants.

Phone calls and personal interviews at work should be carried out from a place of positive energies. Storage areas are less important.

ELEVEN

Afterword

We can never totally banish negative feelings, nor should we, for without them there would be no impetus for change or progress. Nor can or should we deny our shadow side, the feelings and fears we project on to other people or which may haunt our dreams. Psychic protection is based not purely on filtering out all sensation so that we live in perpetual sunlight, but on preventing destructive behaviour by ourselves or others. This behaviour, if left unchecked, may damage our psyche and destroy the innate optimism that we all possessed as children and which can inspire and uplift our spirits as adults.

The process of psychic protection therefore involves transforming darkness into light, sorrow into joy and inertia into positive action. It offers no assurances that we will never again know sorrow or pain, for life is a mixture of rain and sunshine, night and day, shadow and brilliant sunlight. And psychic protection is primarily concerned with living in the real world, not behind a high fence of spiritual seclusion or in some remote island paradise. Indeed, it touches every aspect of our lives. The true message is that if we can gain control over our own fears, we can overcome any threat from others and even from the world beyond.

As I grow older, I realise many of the homilies spoken by my mother, when I was a child, made sound psychic sense: 'Laugh and the world laughs with you', she would say. 'Never let the sun go down on anger.' 'Do unto others as you would have done unto you.' 'Forgive and forget.' 'Never part with bad feeling.' 'Saying sorry costs nothing.' 'If you can't say something nice, don't say anything at all.' 'Count your blessings.'

My mother, who lived and died in the industrialised Midlands of England and whose height of joy was spending a fortnight in a caravan in Wales each year with my eternally pessimistic father, was an unlikely guru, but she had positivity written through her like a stick of Blackpool rock, even on the rainiest of life's cloudy days.

When sorrow or injustice strikes or we are paralysed by fear, it is not easy to be positive. But I do believe that the more joyous and benign the feelings we release into the cosmos by our words and deeds, the happier and more blessed our world will become. If we smile in London in the morning, the smile really does reach Tokyo by nightfall. The greatest form of psychic protection is to give of ourselves and our time freely, not in the hope that it will be returned threefold. What is more, it is important to make at least a little happiness for ourselves every single day and to value every day that does bring joy as it is, rather than frittering away the golden moments by demanding promises of permanency and cast-iron certainties.

Life is intrinsically good. The majority of people are kind and well-meaning, even if – like you and me – they don't always get it right.

Tonight, wherever you are, just before you get ready for bed, light a candle and say some encouraging words into the flame. Recall the happiest moment in your life, your pride in a family member or friend who performed a noble or just amazingly clever deed. Visualise something extraordinary, a scene of great natural beauty, a sunset, a baby's smile, the miracle of birth. Relive the joy of first love and weave the dreams you still hope to fulfil.

Make a promise that tomorrow you will do something, however small, to improve your own fragment of the earth's surface and send a message of reconciliation through the candle to someone who did you wrong. Smile, laugh with them and perhaps even share that precious secret you have been holding close for such an occasion, that million-dollar idea that is going to make you rich and the world a better place.

Now blow out the candle, letting the light, full of joy and good feelings, fly away across the world, shedding light beams as it is amplified by the light of other candles in other places and even from other times.

Sit in the darkness and visualise similar shimmering spheres returning to you from – who knows where or when? Listen to the triumphs and wishes of these unknown people – there is room enough for everyone's brilliant ideas and dreams to be realised. You are part of the cosmic exchange of energies and you are protected by a whole universe of light and positive feelings. You need not fear darkness ever again.

Further Reading

Amulets and Talismans

Migene Gonzalez-Wipler, *The Complete Guide to Amulets and Talismans*, Llewellyn, St Paul, Minnesota, 1991

William Thomas and Kate Pavitt, *The Book of Talismans, Amulets and Zodiacal Gems*, Kessinger, New York, 1998

Auras

Ted Andrews, *How to Read and See the Aura*, Llewellyn, St Paul, Minnesota, 1996

Cassandra Eason, *Auras*, Piatkus, 2000

Mark Smith and Raymond A Moody Jnr, *Auras: See Them in Only 60 Seconds*, Llewellyn, St Paul, Minnesota, 1997

Candle Magic

Ray Buckland, *Advanced Candle Magic*, Llewellyn, St Paul, Minnesota, 1996

Cassandra Eason, *Candle Power*, Blandford, 1999

Chakras

Shafica Karagulla and Dora Van Gelder Kunz, *Chakras and the Human Energy Field*, Theosophical University Press, 1994

Naomi Ozaniec, *The Elements of the Chakras*, Element, 1989

Crystals

Luc Bourgault, *The American Indian Secrets of Crystal Healing*, Quantum, 1997

Scott Cunningham, *The Encyclopaedia of Crystal, Gem and Metal Magic*,

Llewellyn, St Paul, Minnesota, 1991

Curses, the Evil Eye and Psychic Protection

William Bloom, *Psychic Protection*, Piatkus, 1998

Alan Dundee, *The Evil Eye: A Folklore Casebook*, Garland Publishing, Inc., New York, 1981

Dion Fortune, *Psychic Self-Defense*, Aquarian, 1988

Dowsing and Black Streams

Arthur Bailey, *Anyone Can Dowse for Better Health*, Quantum, 1999

Sig Lonegren, *Spiritual Dowsing*, Gothic Images, 1986

Feng Shui

Wendy Hobson, *Simply Feng Shui*, Quantum, 1999

Karen Kingston, *Creating Sacred Space with Feng Shui*, Piatkus, 1999

Flowers, Trees and Plants

Peter Tompkins and Christopher Bird, *The Secret Life of Plants*, Avon Books, New York, 1974

Robert Graves, *The White Goddess*, Faber and Faber, 1988

Flower Remedies

Julian Barnard, *A Guide to the Bach Flower Remedies*, CW Daniel Co., 1992

Andreas Korte, *Orchids, Gemstones and the Healing Energies*, Bauer Verlag, 1993

Clare G Harvey and Amanda Cochrane, *The Encyclopaedia of Flower Remedies*, Thorsons/HarperCollins, 1995

Goddesses

Elinor Gadon, *The Once and Future Goddess*, Aquarian/Thorsons, 1990

Z Budapest, *The Holy Book of Women's Mysteries*, Harper Row, New York, 1990

Ghosts

Cassandra Eason, *Ghost Encounters*, Blandford, 1997

John and Anne Spencer, *The Encyclopaedia of Ghosts and Spirits*, Headline, 1992

Incenses and Oils

Scott Cunningham, *The Complete Book of Oils, Incenses and Brews*, Llewellyn, St Paul, Minnesota, 1991

Gerena Dunwich, *Wicca Garden, A Witch's Guide to Magical and Enchanted Herbs and Plants*, Citadel, 1996

Healing

Barbara Brennan, *Hands of Light*, Bantam Books, 1987

Donna Eden, *Energy Medicine*, Piatkus, 1999

Herbalism

Scott Cunningham, *The Encyclopaedia of Herbs*, Llewellyn, St Paul, Minnesota, 1997

Frank J Lipp, *Herbalism*, Macmillan, 1996

Poltergeists

Alan Gauld and Tony Cornell, *Poltergeists*, Routledge and Kegan Paul, 1979

Guy Lyon, Playfair, *This House is Haunted*, Souvenir Press, 1980

Psychic Children

Cassandra Eason, *The Psychic Power of Children*, Foulsham, 1994

Linda Williamson, *Children and the Spirit World*, Piatkus, 1999

Pyramid Energies

Peter Lemesurier, *Gods of the Dawn: The Message of the Pyramids and the True Stargate Mystery*, Thorsons, 1998

Runes

Paul B Taylor and WH Auden (translators),*The Elder Edda. A Selection from the Icelandic*, Faber and Faber, 1973

Edred Thorsson, *At the Well of Wyrd, A Handbook of Runic Divination*, Samuel Weiser, Maine,1988

Telepathy and Psychokinesis

Hans Eysenck and Carl Sargent, *Explaining the Unexplained*, Weidenfeld and Nicolson, 1982

Joseph Rhine, *The Reach of the Mind*, William Morrow, New York, 1947

Using Parchment and Vellum

Jonathan G Alexander, *Medieval Illuminators and Their Methods of Work*, New Haven, Yale University Press, 1992

Heather Child (editor), *The Calligrapher's Handbook*, Taplinger Publishing Company, 1994

Witchcraft History

Robin Briggs, *Witches and Neighbours, The Social and Cultural Context of European Witchcraft*, HarperCollins, 1996

Rosemary Ellen Guiley, *An Encyclopaedia of Witches and Witchcraft ,Facts on File*, New York, 1989

Useful Contacts

Amulets, Candles, Incenses, etc.

Australia
Future Pastimes
24a Collins Street,
Kiama,
New South Wales
General supplies by mail order.

UK
Pentagram
11 Cheapside,
Wakefield,
WF1 2SD
International mail order and personal sales; New Age, Wiccan and occult.

Crystals

Australia
The Mystic Trader
125 Flinders Lane,
Melbourne 3000
Mail order and personal service.

South Africa
The Wellstead
1 Wellington Avenue,
Wynberg,
Cape 7300
Mail order supplies.

Topstone Mining Corporation CC
Dido Valley Road,
PO Box 20,
Simonstown 7975

UK
The Mystic Trader
60 Chalk Farm Road,
London,
NW1 8AN
Mail order supplies.

Mysteries
7 Monmouth Street,
London,
WC2H 9DA
Shop and mail order; everything for the New Age, plus good advice.

US
Eye of the Cat
3314 East Broadway,
Long Beach,
CA 90803
Mail order crystals and other New Age commodities.

The Crystal Cave
415 West Foothill Blvd,
Claremont,
CA 91711
Mail order. A huge variety of crystal and stones, including unusual ones.

Earth energies

UK
British Society of Dowsers
Sycamore Barn,
Hastingleigh,
Ashford,
Kent,
TN25 5HW

US
The American Society of Dowsers
Dowsers Hall,
Danville,
Vermont, 05828-0024

Feng shui

Australia
Feng Shui Society of Australia
PO Box 1565,
Rozelle,
Sydney,
New South Wales 2039

UK
The Geomancer
The Feng Shui Store,
PO Box 250,
Woking,
Surrey,
GU21 1YJ

Feng Shui Association
11 Woburn Place,
Brighton,
West Sussex,
BN1 9GA

Feng Shui Network International
PO Box 9,
Pateley Bridge,
North Yorkshire,
HG3 5XG
Information and courses.

US
The Feng Shui Institute of America
PO Box 488,
Walbasso,
Fl 32970

Feng Shui Warehouse
PO Box 3005,
San Diego,
CA 92163

Findhorn

UK
Findhorn Foundation
The Park,
Findhorn,
Forres,

Scotland,
IV36 OTZ
Workshops and courses that teach about meditation, consciousness and nature spirits. Also sell flower essences.

Flower remedies

Australia
The Australian Flower Remedy Society
PO Box 531,
Spit Junction,
New South Wales 2007

Australian Native Tree Essences
Sabian,
PO Box 527,
Kew,
Victoria 3101
or The Sabian Centre,
11 Selbourne Road,
Kew,
Victoria 31011

Canada
Pacific Essences
PO Box 8317,
Victoria,
V8W 3R9

Europe
Deva Essences
Korte Phi Essenzen Orkid,
Alpenstrasse 25,
D-78262 Gailingen,
Germany

UK
Bailey Essences
7–8 Nelson Road,
Ilkley,
West Yorkshire,
LS29 8HH

Healing Herbs Ltd
PO Box 65,
Hereford,
HR2 0UW
For Bach Flower Remedies, books and information.

Dr Bach Healing Centre
Mount Vernon,
Solwell,

Wallingford,
Oxfordshire,
OX10 0PZ

US
Alaskan Flower Essence Project
PO Box 1329,
Homer,
AL99603

Bach Flower Remedies,
Nelson Bach,
US Dept NJ95,
1007 West Upsal Street,
Philadelphia,
PA 19119

Desert Alchemy
PO Box 44189,
Tucson,
AZ 85733

Herbs

Australia
The National Herbalists Association of
Australia
PO Box 65,
Kingsgrove,
NSW 2208

UK
Vicki and Ian Foss
Sunacre,
The Terrace,
Chale,
Ventnor,
Isle of Wight,
Hampshire,
PO38 2HL
Wide variety of culinary and medicinal
herbs. Send SAE for list.

The Herb Society
PO Box 599,
London,
SW11 4BW

Gerard House
736 Christchurch Road,
Bournemouth,
Hampshire,
BH7 6BZ
Mail order for dried herbs.

Island Herbs
G Baldwin and Co.,
171–173 Walworth Road,
London,
SE17 1RW
Largest range of herbs and herbal
products in the UK with an extensive mail
order service.

The National Institute of Medical
Herbalists
56 Longbrook Street,
Exeter,
Devon,
EX4 6AH

US
The American Herbalists Guild
PO Box 1683,
Soquel,
CA 95073

The Sage Garden
PO Box 144,
Payette,
ID 83661
Herbs, oils, amulets, incenses by mail order.

Meditation, visualisation and music

UK
Beechwood Music
Littleton House,
Littleton Road,
Ashford,
Middlesex,
TW15 1UU
Stress Busters, music of pan pipes,
rainforest, surf and whales.

The School of Meditation
158 Holland Park Avenue,
London,
W11 4UH

US
Raven Recordings
744 Broad Street,
Room 1815,
Newark,
New Jersey 07102
Meditation music, videos and tapes.

Mediumship and spiritualism

Australia
Australian Spiritualist Association
PO Box 248,
Canterbury 2193,
New South Wales

Canada
Spiritualist Church of Canada
1835 Lawrence Ave East,
Scarborough,
Ontario,
M1R 2Y3

Survival Research Institute of Canada
Walter J Meyer zu Erpen,
PO Box 8697,
Victoria, BC,
V8W 3S3
Publishes *The Directory of Spiritualist Organisations in Canada*, which can be obtained by sending $5 Canadian (or equivalent).

UK
Spiritualist Association of Great Britain
33 Belgrave Square,
London,
SW1 8QL

The Arthur Findlay College and Spiritualist National Union
Stanstead Hall,
Stanstead,
Mountfitchet,
Essex,
CM24 8UD

Paganism

Australia
Novocastrian Pagan Information Centre
Laren, PO Box 129,
Stockton,
New South Wales 2295

The Pagan Alliance
PO Box 823,
Bathurst,
New South Wales 2795
An umbrella movement for pagan organisations.

UK
The Pagan Federation
PO Box 7097,
London,
WC1N 3XX

Parapsychology, psychic study societies and colleges

Eire
Irish UFO/Paranormal Research Association
PO Box 3070,
Whitehall,
Dublin 9

UK
Association for the Scientific Study of Anomalous Phenomena
Dr Hugh Pincott,
St Aldhelm,
20 Paul Street,
Frome,
Somerset,
BA11 1DX

The Churches Fellowship for Spiritual and Psychic Studies
The Rural Workshop,
South Road,
North Somercotes,
near Louth,
Lincolnshire,
LN11 7BT

The College of Psychic Studies
16 Queensberry Place,
London,
SW7 2EB

Fountain International
35 Padacre Road,
Torquay,
Devon,
TQ2 8PX
An organisation that hopes to improve the world through meditation, crystals and spiritual awareness.

The Ghost Club
Tom Perrott,
93 The Avenue,
Muswell Hill,
London,
N10 2QG

Founded in 1862.

Haunted Scotland
35 South Dean Road,
Kilmarnock,
KA3 7RD,
Ayrshire
A bi-monthly magazine produced by Mark and Hannah Fraser who will also help with any ghost sightings, problems with hauntings, etc. They are always glad to receive accounts from anywhere in the world but especially Scotland.

The Scottish Society for Psychical Research
Daphne Plowman,
131 Stirling Drive,
Bishopbriggs,
Glasgow,
G64 3AX

US
American Society for Psychical Research
5 West 73rd Street,
New York,
NY 10023

Ghost Trackers Journal
Box 205,
Oaklawn,
IL 60454

Parapsychology Foundation Counselling Bureau
228 East 71st Street,
New York
NY 10021

Spiritual healing

Canada
National Federation of Spiritual Healers (Canada)
Toronto,
Ontario

UK
British Alliance of Healing Associations
Mrs Jo Wallace,
3 Sandy Lane,
Gisleham,
Lowestoft,
Suffolk,
NR33 8EQ

National Federation of Spiritual Healers
Old Manor Farm Studio,
Church Street,
Sunbury-on-Thames,
Middlesex,
TW16 6RG

US
World of Light
PO Box 425,
Wappingers Falls,
NY 12590
Will send a list of healers.

Wiccan and goddess organisations

Eire
Fellowship of Isis
Huntington Castle,
Bunclody,
Enniscorthy,
Eire
International network of goddess worshippers.

US
Circle Sanctuary
PO Box 219,
Mount Horeb,
WI 53572
Contacts with 700 pagan groups and networks.

Covenant of the Goddess
PO Box 1226,
Berkeley,
California 94704

Living Wicca Foundation
PO Box 4186,
Dunellen,
New Jersey 08812
Founded to continue the work of the late Scott Cunningham.

The Witches' Voice Inc.
PO Box 4924,
Clearwater,
Florida 33758 4924
A resource organisation with worldwide links.

Index